W9-BDQ-600

Trojan Women
Helen
Hecuba

Publication of this volume has been made possible in part
through the generous support and enduring vision of

Warren G. Moon.

TROJAN WOMEN
HELEN
HECUBA

*Three Plays about Women
and the Trojan War*

EVRIPIDES

Verse translations by

Francis Blessington,

with introductions and notes

The University of Wisconsin Press

The University of Wisconsin Press
1930 Monroe Street, 3rd Floor
Madison, Wisconsin 53711-2059
uwpress.wisc.edu

3 Henrietta Street, Covent Garden
London WC2E 8LU, United Kingdom
eurospanbookstore.com

Copyright © 2015
The Board of Regents of the University of Wisconsin System
All rights reserved. Except in the case of brief quotations embedded in critical articles
and reviews, no part of this publication may be reproduced, stored in a retrieval system,
transmitted in any format or by any means—digital, electronic, mechanical, photo-
copying, recording, or otherwise—or conveyed via the Internet or a website without
written permission of the University of Wisconsin Press. Rights inquiries should be
directed to rights@uwpress.wisc.edu.

Printed in the United States of America

This book may be available in a digital edition

Library of Congress Cataloging-in-Publication Data

Euripides, author.
[Works. Selections. English. 2015]
Trojan women, Helen, Hecuba: three plays about women and the Trojan War /
Euripides ; verse translations by Francis Blessington, with introductions and notes.
pages   cm. — (Wisconsin studies in classics)
Includes bibliographical references and index.
ISBN 978-0-299-30524-6 (pbk.: alk. paper)
1. Euripides—Translations into English.
2. Helen, of Troy, Queen of Sparta—Drama.
3. Hecuba, Queen of Troy—Drama.   4. Trojan War—Drama
5. Mythology, Greek—Drama.   I. Blessington, Francis C., 1942–, translator.
II. Euripides. Trojan women. English (Blessington)
II. Euripides. Helen. English (Blessington)
IV. Euripides. Hecuba. English (Blessington)
V. Title.   VI. Series: Wisconsin studies in classics.
PA3975.A2   2015
882'.01—dc23
2015010084

For
Ann
Geoff
Julia

Contents

Acknowledgments

I owe thanks to the following readers who read the whole, or parts, of the manuscript: Professor Guy Rotella of Northeastern University, Professors Richard Elia, Thomas Luddy, and Ann Taylor, my wife, of Salem State University. Thanks also to Lisa McGonagle for information on the law.

I am grateful to the New England Poetry Club for awarding my translation of *Trojan Women* the Der-Hovanessian Prize for the best translation in 2011 and to *Literary Imagination* for publishing a choral ode (lines 511–567) from this play as "The Fall of Troy."

I first translated the *Trojan Women* at the suggestion of Meg Taintor, artistic director for the Whistler in the Dark Theatre Company, for a production in their 2011–2012 season. My gratitude to her and director Ben Evett and the company who participated in the staged reading and in the production. Special gratitude also to Professor Hugh K. Long for performing my translation of *Trojan Women* at Athens State University in 2013.

Euripides:
"The Philosopher of the Stage"

The tragedies of Euripides challenged those of his predecessors. If Aeschylus found that there was justice in the world, even if delayed, and Sophocles saw that man ironically could destroy himself by pursuing Greek values too far, Euripides challenged the rational foundation of civilized life itself, the philosophical basis of Plato and Aristotle. His plays investigate how futile ideas and ideals can be. But Euripides presents no easy answers. Conflicting sides have their valid claims, though not always equally right. His characters, like Hecuba, may challenge the justice of, even the existence of, the gods, but she claims we still need them.

Euripides' audience was made up of the sophisticated citizens of the polis (city-state), and his subject matter was often either that of the heroic era portrayed by Homer three centuries earlier or that of traditional mythology. Yet his Heracles was not the great hero of the labors but rather a man driven by madness to kill his wife and three children. He is reduced from a hero to a man who needs a friend like Theseus just to continue living. Euripides' characters are always at the extremes of life: a woman in a bacchic frenzy tears apart her son; another plots and kills her children out of jealousy at being abandoned by her husband; a god destroys a royal family because he is not worshipped; a woman is rescued from captivity and the danger of rape, and her long-lost husband saved from imminent death by the gods.

The triumph of the irrational, both tragic and benign, was often his theme. His interest in the emotional side of human nature led him to investigate war and women's roles in warring societies. Homer presented war directly, but Euripides dramatizes its aftermath in these three plays. He saw that the masculine society of ancient Greece was emotionally entwined with the opposite sex: A woman was said to have caused the Trojan War, and women suffered the consequences long after many of the heroes were dead. Female concerns—family, identity, slavery, revenge, justice, knowledge, intelligence, religion, love, and hate—were the concerns of Euripides' modern city-state that had passed beyond the Homeric world but had to cross-examine its values. Is Hecuba's revenge morally just in Euripides' time? Is Helen's benevolent world possible? Is Hecuba's endurance the true heroism? These are questions for our world, too. The popularity of Euripides today demonstrates how fundamental his plays are to human experience.

Principal Dates in the Life of Euripides

Euripides is said to have written ninety-two plays, of which nineteen survive under his name, the largest number of any ancient Greek dramatist. There are two main medieval manuscripts: one of ten plays used in schools with scholia (ancients commentaries) and nine (without scholia) from an alphabetical collection (only H through K). At least seventeen tragedies are considered certainly by Euripides. *Rhesus* (date unknown) is disputed, and *Cyclops* is a satyr play (lighter drama). Some fragments also have survived.

485 (480?)	Born on the island of Salamis near Athens or at Phyla (?).
480	Persians sack Athens. Athens defeats them in the Battle of Salamis.
469	Birth of Socrates, the philosopher and friend of Euripides.
456	Death of the tragedian Aeschylus.
455 (?)	First play, now lost, *The Peliades*.
447–432	Parthenon built during the Age of Pericles.
441	First prize. Play unknown.
438	*Alcestis*.
431	*Medea*. Peloponnesian War begins between Athens and Sparta for the leadership of Greece and lasts till the defeat of Athens in 404.

430 (?)   *Children of Heracles*. Plague in Athens.

429   Pericles dies in the plague.

428   *Hippolytus*.

425 (?)   *Andromache*.

424 (?)   *Hecuba*.

423 (?)   *Suppliant Women*.

420 (?)   *Electra*.

416 (?)   *Heracles*.

415   *Trojan Women*. Athenian attempt to annex Sicily fails miserably. Sicilians, said to have been charmed by the songs of Euripides, release Athenian prisoners.

414 (?)   *Iphigenia in Tauris*.

413 (?)   *Ion*.

412   *Helen*.

411–409   *Phoenician Women*.

408 (?)   *Orestes, Cyclops*. Euripides goes to the Court of Agelaus at Pella in Macedonia.

407/406 (?)   Iphigenia in Aulis. Dies at Pella. *Bacchae* produced posthumously. Death of rival playwright Sophocles.

404   End of Peloponnesian War and fall of Athens.

Note on the Translations

The thrill of translating Euripides is to follow the associations of Euripides' mind. Besides the usual obstacles of corruptions in the text, the translator of Euripides who aims at a general audience faces some difficulties: what to do with compound words, exclamations, and interjections, and how not to produce a lower level of diction than the general reader may reasonably expect. These must be balanced by the familiar expectations of English poetry. Compound words can clutter English lines and so must be seldom used. Exclamations and interjections are often word music in Greek *otototototoi* (*Trojan Women*, 1287) of unknown origin, but in English, they often have echoes of Christianity, as in the overpopular "Oh My God" (OMG). I have chosen more sophisticated versions of the latter rather than interrupt the flow of English with transliterations from Greek. The style of Euripides is somewhat lower than Aeschylus and Sophocles, but not as low as some translations have brought it. I have tried to indicate the formality and rhetoric of the Greek text without sounding "literary." In the notes (which are keyed to line numbers), I not only identify historical and mythological names and places but also indicate specifically Greek themes and contexts so the reader may better understand the overtones and issues in the plays. I have also tried to stimulate literary analysis without overemphasizing the obvious.

Greek tragedy combines lines of dialogue in iambic trimeters (three pairs, or *metra*, of iambic verse, or six iambic feet, with variations) with passages of more irregular lyric measures, often sung. In the choral odes, the stanzas are divided into strophe (turn), antistrophe (counter-turn), and sometimes epode (after-song). The strophe and antistrophe correspond metrically. In English, I have tried to find equivalents that would bring the reader closer to the Greek original rather than duplicating Greek meters in English, because of the different metrical uses in the two languages. For example, the dochmius ($\smile$ — — $\smile$ —) is often used in tragedy to increase emotion, positively or negatively, but would have little effect in English. Iambs fit dialogue, both in Greek and English, but dactyls and anapests imply light verse in English, while the dactyl suggests heroic verse in Greek, and anapests, originally a marching meter, can be used for tragic songs, character introductions, and exits. For flexibility, I have used a four-beat variable stress line for the Greek dialogue's iambic trimeters and freer verse for the lyrical parts, where Euripides uses many lyrical meters with frequent variations because many passages were sung and because of the highly emotional nature of his plays. I have kept the metrical correspondence of strophe and antistrophe. Overall, I have tried to produce a contemporary poetic idiom that can be read, performed, and taught today.

TROJAN WOMEN

Introduction

Why sing in hell? What do you sing in hell?

Euripides' *Trojan Women* (*Troades*) explores, with rare depth, human suffering and human identity. The women of the title are awaiting the Greek ships to carry them to slavery after their men have been slaughtered. The backstory is well known. The Trojan prince Paris, also called Alexander, judged a beauty contest among three goddesses: Hera, Athena, and Aphrodite. Hera and Athena tried to bribe him with military power, but Aphrodite offered the most beautiful woman in the world, Helen of Troy. Following Paris' carrying off Helen from Sparta, the Greeks, led by her husband, Menelaus, and his brother, Agamemnon, besieged Troy for ten years. They finally captured the city by building a wooden horse and filling it with soldiers. Believing the horse an omen of good fortune, the Trojans brought it into the city and lost the war and their city.

Since its first performance in 415 BC, Euripides' play has been applauded on the stage but has presented problems for modern critics. Is it a cautionary tale against war? Does it reflect the Athenian massacre of Melos in 416? Or their self-destructive Sicilian invasion of 415? Is it just a series of loosely connected scenes of pathos? Is it one long scream against the unbearable horrors of fate, part of Euripides' "most unmitigated misery ever witnessed on a stage" (E. Segal, *Oxford Readings*, 244)? Is this what Aristotle really meant by calling Euripides "the most tragic of poets" (*Poetics*, 1453a)? Does nothing redeem the misery? Why then did it influence Roman writers like Ennius and Accius and inspire Seneca's greatest play? Why does it have ever-popular modern performances and adaptations? Note the film version of 1971 by Michael Cacoyannis.

Modern scholars have stressed the play's original context as one part of a probably connected trilogy, the form used by

Aeschylus years before, then revived by Euripides. Although fragments of the other two plays have survived, we are missing many details. About AD 200, Aelian writes that Xenocles, "whoever in the world that is," won first prize in 415 and "second to him was Euripides with *Alexandros, Palamedes, Trojan Women*, and the satyr-play *Sisyphus*" (Kovacs, *Euripidea*, 428). The first play deals with the story of Alexander and the prophecy that he would be a "firebrand" to destroy Troy. He is to die by exposure, but he is rescued and brought up by slaves. His parents think he is dead. He returns to the court and defeats his brothers in an athletic contest. Thinking they were bested by a slave, his brother Deiphobus and his mother Hecuba plan to kill him, but somehow Cassandra discovers his identity and he is reinstated as a prince of Troy.

The second play features Palamedes, the inventor of writing, who had once discovered the trick by which Odysseus had tried to avoid going to the Trojan War. In this play, Odysseus, out of revenge, plants some money under Palamedes' tent and accuses him of selling out the Greek army. He is killed for treason. His brother, Oeax, alerts their father, Nauplius, by writing on oar blades and throwing them into the ocean. Later, his father tricks and destroys the returning Greek fleet by setting up false signal fires on the coast of Euboea.

Is Troy then destroyed because Priam and Hecuba did not kill their child? When Poseidon and Athena agree at the beginning of *Trojan Women* to destroy the returning Greek fleet because Ajax has violated Athena's temple, are they also avenging what Odysseus did to Palamedes, so that the conquerors as well as the conquered are punished? That might be true if Aeschylus or Sophocles wrote the play. But with Euripides we are not sure. Should, or could, Priam and Hecuba kill their newborn child? Are the gods unfair?

Or *are* there gods? Hecuba's prayer is typical of Euripides' employing the gods and questioning them at the same time:

O support of earth, having your seat on earth—
Zeus, or air—whoever you are, difficult to know,
Either necessity of nature or mind of man,
I pray to you. In silent ways,
You lead all mortal affairs to justice. (884–888)

The play opens with an agreement between Poseidon and
Athena to destroy the victorious Greek fleet, a prophecy we
must keep in mind as the play progresses because, gods or not,
it came true, but *after* the action of the play. This retribution
may imply the justice that Hecuba longs for. Within the action,
we see no retribution, only the suffering of the women and
their reactions. Two other relevant fates also occur after the
play, and the Greek audience was aware of them. Hecuba, taken
as a slave by Odysseus, never reaches his homeland of Ithaca. She
is changed into a mad dog and leaps from the mast of the ship to
an ocean death (cf. *Hecuba*, 1259–1273). Helen, taken back to
Sparta supposedly to die, becomes the complacent housewife
who breezily tells her tale in Homer's *Odyssey* (4.235–289). All
three extraneous events affect us as we watch or read this tragedy.

The destruction of Melos occurred a few months before the
play. The Athenians destroyed the city, massacred the men,
and sold the women and children into slavery. The play is often
read as a protest against this atrocity and against the planned
Sicilian Expedition that turned out so disastrously later in 415
(Murray, *Euripides and His Age*, 63–65), but there are no references to Melos in the play or to the Sicilian Expedition. Perhaps
Euripides did not have enough time to write a Melian play and
rehearse a chorus (Kip, "Euripides and Melos"). Even if he did,
such horrors were all too common in the ancient Greek world.
Such a protest seems to jar against the praise of Athens within
the play and against classical Athenian ideology (Sidwell, "Melos
and the *Trojan Women*").

Is the play a general condemnation or critique of war, as it
is often read (Murray, *Euripides and His Age*; Sartre, "Why the

Trojan Women?"; Vellacott, *Ironic Drama*; Croally, *Euripidean Polemic*)? Surely the suffering of war is the subject, and in 415 BC many felt that Athens was courting destruction by deciding to extend its empire to Sicily, a prediction that turned out to be unfortunately true. At the same time, Athens was still at war with Sparta and had been for fifteen years. But war was a constant condition of ancient Greek life. Poseidon condemns only excessive and irreligious violations committed in war, not war itself:

Foolish is the man who plunders cities,
Temples, and tombs, the sacred places of the dead.
Bringing havoc, he will be destroyed. (95–97)

And Cassandra reveals that just wars are those fought on behalf of a city-state:

He who thinks well must avoid war.
If it comes, to die nobly is not a shameful crown
For the city, but to die ignobly is a disgrace. (400–402)

The cruelties of war are the subject of the play, but we must seek further for its theme. One complication is that we cannot say that there is no humanity in the play if we follow carefully the reactions of the herald, Talthybius (Gilmartin, "Talthybius"). On the other hand, to trace the cause or origin of the suffering leads us to gods who might not exist. Instead of the sense of divine justice in the world that might characterize a play by Aeschylus or Sophocles, we find a dialectic that questions without answering directly. The Greeks in general might be the villains, but they do not appear on stage.

In the play, Euripides presents the issue of the cause of the war in a "trial" scene between Helen and Hecuba (914–1032). The supposed cause of the war, Helen, confronts the greatest living victim of the war, Hecuba. Helen presents her defense in essay form (*rhesis*), followed by Hecuba's rebuttal. Helen was often seen in Euripides' time as a whore, but she was also considered a victim. The tale of her flight with Paris leaves open her complicity: runaway or abductee?

Defenses of Helen focus on her as a victim of Zeus' plan to reduce the human population (the *Cypria*). The orator, Gorgias, wrote a seemingly lighthearted defense of Helen. Gorgias claims that she was the victim of the gods, love, force, and rhetoric (*Encomium of Helen*). Helen uses these arguments in the play. To a modern audience, they might appear sophistical, but many ancient Greeks still believed in the Homeric gods and their mysterious ways of working and causing human suffering. "The will of Zeus was accomplished" (*Iliad*, 1.5). These arguments are no more farfetched than today's that blame God's plan, evolution, or political determinism to explain tragedy. The argument that Helen never went to Troy at all is not mentioned in *Trojan Women* but could have been in the minds of the audience (cf. "Introduction" to *Helen* in this volume). Nevertheless, blaming the gods never acquitted even Greeks of the heroic age from all responsibility (Adkins, *Merit*, 16). In Euripides' time, Athens was moving toward rationalism as it shifted away from the world of Homer to that of the polis (city-state).

Helen claims that Hecuba should have killed Paris as a baby because she dreamed he was a firebrand who would destroy the city, an argument that was echoed by Andromache in the play (597) and formed part of the first play in this trilogy, *Alexandros*. The idea is not so unrealistic if we remember Sophocles' Oedipus. Like a good dramatist, Euripides avoids simplicity by building up both sides of the argument; the audience can decide.

Euripides may have started as a painter and is noted for his imagery (Barlow, *Imagery of Euripides*, 15). One of the dominant images in the play is that of feet: dancing feet, marching feet,

stumbling feet. Poseidon opens with a reference to the perfect
dance of the sea nymphs, the Nereids:

I, Poseidon, have come, leaving
The salty depth of the sea, where Nereids
Turn their shining feet in dance. (1–3)

From this symbol of perfection, we degenerate to the broken
Hecuba, whose song has lost the dance:

And even this is music to the wretched:
To sing their ruin without the dance. (120–121)

She remembers the days when she led the dance:

I'll raise the cry,
Not the same dance song
I raised for Troy's gods once,
When the scepter supported Priam,
And my foot was first in the dance
With loud Phrygian steps. (147–152)

Cassandra tries to convince her mother, Hecuba, to dance, for
Cassandra will avenge Troy by provoking the murder of
Agamemnon, Troy's conqueror, thus bringing down his royal
Greek house. The dance has been restored:

Swing your foot high, bring the chorus
—Evoe!—
As in the happiest days of my father.
Holy is the chorus!
Lead, Phoebus. In your temple and crowned with sweet bay,
I sacrifice.
O Hymen, Hymen, Lord of Brides!

Now dance, mother, the lead.
Turn your feet, here and there, with mine
in lovely steps. (325-334)

Hecuba cannot fathom her daughter's prophecy, true as it is. Hecuba's feet are old, leaden, beaten:

And whom will I serve, I who need
In my old hand a stick for a third foot? (275-276)

Lead my foot, graceful in Troy once,
A slave now, to my bed of leaves on the ground
And my stony pillow, so falling I shall perish. (506-508)

Her foot does not quicken until she forces herself to bid good-bye to Troy:

But, old foot, hurry as you can,
So I may say good-bye to the dying city. (1275-1276)

If the *Trojan Women* opens with the perfect dance, it ends with a forced march. The chorus closes the play with:

March to the Achaean ships! (1332)

It would be too easy to say that the suffering in the play has been resolved into acceptance. As we shall know by the end, too much has happened dramatically and has been said lyrically to see the ending as a solution, or even a real resolution. The play begins in despair and increases in despair, as hope yields to hopelessness and reality fades to memory and dream. What we witness and experience is the heroic female spirit enduring the worst. Their despair contrasts with the grandeur of some of Euripides' greatest odes, celebrating and lamenting the glory that was Troy. At one hopeful moment, Hecuba believes that Troy will live on in poetry (1242–1245). But later she and the chorus say the name will die (1278, 1319, 1322). We know it will not. Perhaps *we* could not bear the thought. But the characters do not know the future. In their cataclysm of suffering, they endure ignorance and sorrow. For them, hopes rise only to fall in an increasingly dramatic sequence. The human spirit wrestles with dream and fact, grand memory and future pain, madness and grief, hate and love, identity and annihilation. But the human mind goes on living, coping, dreaming, remembering, despairing, changing, thinking, even philosophizing, and doing these activities over again, refusing to fall silent, refusing in its way to die. Formally, and so, aesthetically, these actions are elevated to dialogue, song, ode, and dance. The Dance of Life and the Dance of Death. The mystery of life and its pain have not been simplified but reproduced and amplified. The wonder is that human nature can endure, and express, so much so well. The Trojan women's endurance and their continued spirit are their heroic triumph. Unlike all other Greek characters in Greek tragedy, Hecuba never leaves the stage.

Note on the Greek Text

I have used as my main text James Diggle's Oxford Classical Text, *Euripidis Fabulae*, II (1981). (Line numbering corresponds to Diggle's text, not to my translation.) I have also used these editions:

G. Murray, Euripides, *Euripidis Fabulae*, II (Oxford: Oxford University Press, 1913).
W. Biehl, Euripides, *Troades* (Leipzig: Teubner, 1970).

K. H. Lee, Euripides, *Troades* (London: Macmillan, 1976; 2nd ed. London: Bristol Classical Press, 1997), with commentary.

S. A. Barlow, Euripides, *Trojan Women* (Warminster: Aris and Philips, 1986). J. Diggle's Oxford Classical Text with commentary.

D. Kovacs, Euripides, IV, *Trojan Women, Iphigenia among the Taurians, Ion* (Cambridge, MA: Harvard University Press, 1999).

List of Characters

POSEIDON, God of the Sea

PALLAS ATHENA, a goddess

HECUBA, Queen of Troy and widow of King Priam

CHORUS, captive Trojan women

TALTHYBIUS, a herald

CASSANDRA, a prophetess and daughter of Hecuba

ANDROMACHE, widow of Hector, the son of Hecuba

MENELAUS, King of Sparta

HELEN, Menelaus' wife

ASTYANAX, son of Andromache and Hector (silent part)

> (Before a tent, an old woman lies face down. In the background, Trojan houses are burning, after the conquest by the Greeks. POSEIDON enters.)

POSEIDON:
I, Poseidon, have come, leaving
The salty depth of the sea, where Nereids
Turn their shining feet in dance.
From the time Apollo and I raised up
The stony towers around Troy   5
Straight and true, never has the city

Of my Phrygians been distant from my heart.
Now smoldering, she lies sacked and wasted
By the Achaean spear. The Phocian from Parnassus,
Epeius, with Athena's connivance, built   10
And sent within the towered walls a horse
Pregnant with weaponry, a statue of death
[Which later men shall call "the wooden
Spear-horse," since it bore shafts inside].

The sacred groves are deserted, the dwellings   15
Of the gods flow with murder, and by the altar steps
Of Zeus the Protector, Priam lies dead.
Much gold and Phrygian spoil are hauled
To the Achaean ships that wait for a fair wind
From the stern, so that after ten seed-times   20
Those Greeks who warred down this city
May gladly see their wives and children.
Since I am bested by the Argive goddess Hera,
And by Athena, who both brought down the Trojans,
I'll leave renowned Troy and my altars.   25
For when hateful devastation takes a city,
Religion suffers, and the gods are not honored.

The Scamander resounds with shrieking captives,
Women being allotted their masters.
The Arcadians and the Thessalians have taken some,   30
And the chiefs of the Athenians, Theseus' sons, others.
Those Trojan Women still masterless
Are in this tent and kept for the generals.
With them is Tyndareus' daughter, Spartan
Helen, justly judged a captive.   35

Should anyone wish to look on this wretched woman,
It is Hecuba, lying before the tent, pouring

Out many tears for many reasons.
Unknown to her, her pitiful child
Polyxena lies dead on Achilles' tomb.   40
Priam also is gone and their sons. And the virgin,
Cassandra, whom Lord Apollo left frantic,
Agamemnon will force her to his illicit bed,
Rejecting the god's wish, and piety, too.
So farewell, my once prosperous city   45
Of carved towers. If Athena, the child of Zeus,
Had not destroyed you, you would be still
        standing.

(PALLAS ATHENA enters.)

ATHENA:
May I address the one nearest my father in birth,
A great power and honored by gods,
If I put down my former hatred?   50

POSEIDON:
You may, for family conversations, Lady Athena,
Possess a great charm for the heart.

ATHENA:
I applaud your kind nature and suggest
A course of common interest, my lord.

POSEIDON:
Do you bring a new message from the gods,   55
From Zeus, or some lesser deity?

ATHENA:
No—but on account of Troy, where we stand,
I came to join your power to mine.

POSEIDON:
Surely you do not toss aside your hate
And pity Troy burned to ash?   60

ATHENA:
Back to my point. Will you share my plan
And agree to what I wish to do?

POSEIDON:
Of course. But I want to know your mind.
Are you on the Achaean side or the Trojan?

ATHENA:
I wish to cheer the Trojans I once hated   65
And give a bitter return to the Achaean army.

POSEIDON:
Why do you leap about like this, hating
And loving too much anyone you meet?

ATHENA:
Don't you know they violated me and my shrines?

POSEIDON:
Yes. When Ajax took Cassandra by force.   70

ATHENA:
He suffered nothing at Achaean hands, not a word.

POSEIDON:
But they sacked Troy under your power!

ATHENA:
I want us to bring disaster on them.

POSEIDON:
I'm ready to do as you wish. What will you do?

ATHENA:
Give them a homecoming that is no homecoming!   75

POSEIDON:
When they are on land, or on the salt sea?

ATHENA:
When they sail from Troy to home,
Zeus shall send a storm and terrible
Hail and dark blasts of air.
He says he will give me fiery lightning   80
To strike the Achaeans and burn the ships.
You, for your part, bring the Aegean
Raging in grand, whirling waves.
Fill the hollow depth of Euboea with corpses
So that from now on the Achaeans will know   85
To honor my temples and the other gods.

POSEIDON:
So be it. This favor needs few words.
I shall stir up the salty Aegean.
The headlands of Myconos, the hummocks of Delos,
Scyros, Lemnos, and the beaches of Caphareus   90
Will swim with the bodies of many dead.

Go to Olympus and take the thunderbolts
From your father's hand and wait
Till the Achaean fleet is under full sail.
Foolish is the man who plunders cities,   95
Temples, and tombs, the sacred places of the dead.
Bringing havoc, he will be destroyed.

(POSEIDON and PALLAS ATHENA exit.)

HECUBA:
Up, desperate one, raise your head
And neck from the ground. Troy's gone,
And we rule Troy no more.   100
Endure the change of fate.
Sail the passage. Sail your destiny.
Don't set life's prow against
The wave and sail by chance.
Never, never!   105

What's not for me to cry about?
My country, children, husband all have perished.
The grandness of my ancestors
Cut short: how you are nothing now.
Why be silent? Why not?   110
Why lament?
Miserable I am, under a heavy fate
That lies upon my limbs—what torture!
My back stretched on a hard bed.
My head! My temples!   115
My ribs! I wish to pitch
And roll my back and spine
To both sides, always
Weeping elegies in song.
And even this is music to the wretched: 120
To sing their ruin without the dance.

Ships' prows with swift oars,
That came to sacred Troy
Through the purple sea
And Greece's safe harbors,   125
With the pipes' hated war song

And the sweet flutes,
You hung the twisted rope,
Egyptian-grown,
Alas, in Troy's gulfs,   130
Chasing Menelaus'
Hated wife, Castor's disgrace,
The shame of Sparta,
Slaughterer
Of Priam, sower of fifty sons.   135

She has run me, poor Hecuba,
Aground in this disaster.
What seats I sit on
By Agamemnon's tent!
An old woman and a slave,   140
I'm led from home,
My head pitifully mauled by grief.

But, O poor wives
Of the bronze-speared Trojans
And ill-mated brides,
Troy smolders. Let's weep for it!   145
As if I were a mother of young birds,
I'll raise the cry,
Not the same dance song
I raised for Troy's gods once,
When the scepter supported Priam,   150
And my foot was first in the dance
With loud Phrygian steps.

(SEMI-CHORUS A enters from the tent.)

SEMI-CHORUS A:
Hecuba, what are you shouting?

What and why do you call out? Through walls
I heard your grief.   155
Fear shoots through the hearts
Of the Trojan women
Inside who cry out at their slavery.

HECUBA:
O child, hands that carry the oars
Are now moving to the Greek ships.   160

SEMI-CHORUS A:
No, no! What do the Greeks want? Surely they will
Transport me now out of my fatherland.

HECUBA:
I don't know. I'd guess—the worst.

SEMI-CHORUS A:
Please, no!
Poor Trojan women, come out   165
To hear your hard fate:
The Greeks are preparing for home.

HECUBA:
Oh, no,
Don't send out   170
The bacchic Cassandra,
My maenad girl
For Greeks to shame.
I will be grieved then all the more.
O, O
Troy, wretched Troy, you are gone,
And wretched are those who leave you,
The living, and the dead.   175

(SEMI-CHORUS B enters from the tent.)

SEMI-CHORUS B:
Woe on woe, I left that tent there,
Agamemnon's, trembling at your words,
My Queen. Will Greeks
Kill what's left of me?
Are those sailors ready   180
To set their stern oars soon in motion?

HECUBA:
O child, terror-stricken I came,
My soul shuddering before dawn.

SEMI-CHORUS B:
Has some Danaan herald come already?
Who will I lie with, me a wretched slave?   185

HECUBA:
You are near your allotments now.

SEMI-CHORUS B:
No, please!
What Argive man or Phthian
Or islander leads
Unfortunate me far from Troy?

HECUBA:
You gods!   190
In whose land
Shall I live in slavery,
A worn-out rag,
In form a corpse,
The fleeting image of a corpse?
No, no!

Shall I keep guard at a gate,
Or bring up another's child, I   195
Who held the highest rank?

CHORUS:
Alas, with what pitiable outcries
Could you scream out your outrage?
Not by *Trojan* looms will I shift
The spinning shuttle back and forth.   200
One last time, I look at my parents' home—
One last time! I shall have even more suffering:
I shall be brought to a Greek bed
—May that night die with my fate!—
Or wretched slave to fetch the water,   205
From Pirene's sacred fountains.
May I go to Theseus'
Famed and favored country.
But *not* to the swirling Eurotas,   210
Helen's most detested land,
As a slave and meet Menelaus,
The ravisher of Troy!

I heard that blest, beautiful country,
Foundation of Olympus,   215
Land of the Peneus, is lush
With riches and with fruitfulness.
My next best is there after wishing for
That blest country of Theseus: Athens.
I hear the Etnean island,   220
The god Hephaestus' land,
Is heralded for crowns of honor,
A mother of mountains that faces Carthage.
And that land neighboring
The Ionian sea   225
Which Crathis, the finest of rivers,

That dyes hair reddish brown
Nourishes with streams, makes happy
A land of virtuous men.

Now this herald from the army   230
Of the Danaans, a steward of horrible news,
Marches in, stopping his swift steps.
What is he bringing? What is he going to say?
For we are slaves already of a Dorian land.

(TALTHYBIUS enters.)

TALTHYBIUS:
Hecuba, you know me from making   235
Many trips to Troy, the Achaean herald,
Known to you before, lady.
I, Talthybius, have come, bringing news.

HECUBA:
My old fear, my dear women.

TALTHYBIUS:
Your lot is cast, if this was your fear.   240

HECUBA:
No, no.
What city do you say: in Thessaly, Phthia,
Or Cadmus' country?

TALTHYBIUS:
Each of you is allotted a different man.

HECUBA:
Who won whom? What Trojan woman
Has good fortune waiting for her?   245

TALTHYBIUS:
I know. But learn separately. Not all at once.

HECUBA:
My child,
Who won her, tell me, the curst Cassandra?

TALTHYBIUS:
Lord Agamemnon chose her himself.

HECUBA:
A slave for the Laconian   250
Lady—what hell!

TALTHYBIUS:
No, but an illegal marriage for his bed.

HECUBA:
Her, the virgin, to whom golden-haired Apollo
Gave the gift of living untouched?

TALTHYBIUS:
Love's arrow struck him for the possessed girl.   255

HECUBA:
Child, throw away your laurel branches,
And from your skin the divine garment
Of wreaths you wear.

TALTHYBIUS:
Yes, is it not a great thing to succeed to a king's bed?

HECUBA:
What about my youngest you took from me?   260
Where is she?

TALTHYBIUS:
You speak of Polyxena—or who?

HECUBA:
Her, who is her lot?

TALTHYBIUS:
She is set to serve at Achilles' tomb.

HECUBA:
Unlucky me, I bore her a servant to a tomb.   265
But what custom or law of the Greeks
Is this, my friend?

TALTHYBIUS:
Good fortune favors your child. She fares well.

HECUBA:
What are you saying?
Does she still see the sun?   270

TALTHYBIUS:
Fate has her, so she is free of pain.

HECUBA:
What of the wife of Hector, master of war,
Miserable Andromache, what is her fate?

TALTHYBIUS:
She, also, was chosen. Achilles' son took her.

HECUBA:
And whom will I serve, I who need   275
In my old hand a stick for a third foot?

TALTHYBIUS:
Lord Odysseus of Ithaca won you to be his slave.

HECUBA:
Please, no!
Strike your shorn head!
Tear your cheeks with your nails!   280
Ah me—
I drew the lot of slaving
For a rotten deceiver,
Hostile to justice, a lawless beast,
Who twists all things all ways   285
And opposites back again
With his double tongue,
Making what was loved hateful to all.
Screech for me, Trojan Women.
I am cross-starred and ruined,   290
Most wretched in misfortune
And fallen by lot.

CHORUS:
You know your fortune, my queen,
But what Achaean or Hellene holds mine?

TALTHYBIUS:
Go, slaves, we need to bring out
Cassandra as fast as possible and put her   295
Into the hands of the commander-in-chief.
Then I'll lead the chosen captives to the others.

Uh! Why is a pine torch burning inside?
Are the Trojan women firing their tents, or what,
Because they are to be drawn from this land   300
To Argos, and burning their bodies,

Wishing to die? At such times to be sure
Freedom endures evil, though impatient of the yoke.
Open, open up! Don't let what is best for them
And hateful to the Achaeans throw blame on me.   305

HECUBA:
No, they are not burning anything. But my bacchic
Daughter, Cassandra, is rushing here.

(CASSANDRA enters from the tent.)

CASSANDRA:
Raise, present, bring light, I honor
—Look, look!—
And light this temple with torches, Lord Hymen.   310
Blessed is the bridegroom
And blessed am I too with a royal bed
In Argos, married!
O Hymen, Hymen, Lord of Brides!
Since you, mother, with tears,   315
With screams, you cry for father dead
And our loved country,
I light in marriage
My mother's torch   320
To gleam, to shine,
Giving it to you, O Hymen,
Giving you light, O Hecate,
For virgin beds
As custom demands.

Swing your foot high, bring the chorus   325
—Evoe!—
As in the happiest days of my father.
Holy is the chorus!

Lead, Phoebus. In your temple and crowned with sweet
        bay,
I sacrifice.   330
O Hymen, Hymen, Lord of Brides!
Now dance, mother, the lead.
Turn your feet, here and there, with mine
In lovely steps.
Cry—O!—the hymn   335
With blessed tunes,
Cry out the bride!
Go, O Trojans robed for beauty!
Celebrate, sing the fated man
To share my bed   340
In marriage, my bridegroom!

CHORUS:
My queen, won't you seize your raving daughter
Before she runs into the Argive camp?

HECUBA:
Hephaestus, you bring the marriage torch for mortals,
But you fan this fiery misery far
From my grand hopes. No, child,   345
Not with spear point or Argive spear
Did I expect your marriage consummated. Give me
The fire! It's not right you bear a torch,
A raging maenad, nor in misfortune, child,
Have your senses cleared, but stay like this.   350
Bring inside the torches, Trojan women,
Exchange tears for her wedding songs.

CASSANDRA:
Mother, crown my head with victory
And rejoice in my royal marriage.

Escort me, and, even if I am unwilling,   355
Drag me. If Apollo exists,
The famed lord of the Achaeans, Agamemnon,
Marries into a more troublesome marriage than Helen's.
For I will kill him and plunder his house
In return, avenging my brothers and father.   360
But I will stop. I will not sing of the axe
That will enter my neck and other beheadings
And the matricidal agonies that my marriage brings
And the overthrow of the House of Atreus.
I shall show this city more fortunate than the Achaeans,   365
And, though possessed, I shall stand
That much outside my bacchic madness.

For one woman and one love,
They hunted Helen and destroyed thousands.
The *wise* general killed his beloved child   370
On behalf of the hateful and gave up
The pleasures of children at home for his brother,
For a woman willing, and not taken by force.

After they came to the Scamander's banks,
They kept dying, though no one had taken their land   375
Or their high-towers. Those Ares seized
Did not see their children, were not shrouded
By a wife's touch, and lie in an alien land.
Like things happened at home:
Some women died widows; others childless,   380
Having raised children in their homes for nothing.
At their tombs, no one pours the blood offering.
For all this, the army must be *commended*!
Better to be silent about shameful things.
May she who hymns evil be not my muse.   385

First, Trojans—their greatest fame!—
Died for their country, those corpses the spear took
Were borne home by those dear to them
And have a garment of earth in their fatherland,
Wrapped by hand in the required rites.   390
Those Phrygians who did not die in battle
Always lived with wife and children,
Pleasures foreign to the Achaeans.

Hear how it is with Hector, so wretched you think:
He passed away in reputation the best.   395
The coming of the Greeks did that.
Had they stayed home, his valor would have gone
        unnoticed.
Paris married Zeus' daughter, but if he did not,
At home he would have had a wife no one heard of.
He who thinks well must avoid war.   400
If it comes, to die nobly is not a shameful crown
For the city, but to die ignobly is a disgrace.
For this, you should not, mother, pity
Our country or my marriage bed, for by my marriage,
I shall kill those we hate most.   405

CHORUS:
How sweetly you laugh at domestic disasters
And sing what you will perhaps see later is false.

TALTHYBIUS:
Had Apollo not maddened you, you would not
Send out my commanders from the land
With such a prophecy without paying a price.   410
But those thought grand and wise
Are no better than nothing at all:

For the great lord of the Pan-Hellenes,
Atreus' dear son, subjugated himself
And chose the love of this maenad. I'm a poor man   415
But I wouldn't have asked for her bed.

You don't have a sound mind.
Your reproaches to the Argives and praises of the Phrygians
I toss to the winds. Follow me to the ship
—A great match for the general!—And you,   420
When the son of Laertes wants to take you,
Follow him. You will be a slave to a virtuous woman,
So those who came to Troy say.

CASSANDRA:
What a fierce flunky he is. Why do they have
The name "heralds," hateful to all men,   425
Who humor tyrants and city-states? You said
My mother shall go under Odysseus' roof?
Where are the words of Apollo, communicated
To me, that she will die here? I won't insult
Her with the rest. The wretched Odysseus,   430
He does not know what he will suffer.
How my suffering and Troy's will seem gold
To him. Ten years more he will complete
And arrive in his fatherland alone,
[Beyond] the narrow, rocky strait that fierce Charybdis   435
Inhabits, the mountaineering Cyclops,
Who eats flesh raw, and Ligurian Circe,
Transformer of men to swine, and shipwreck at sea,
And the love of lotus and the Sun's sacred cattle
Whose sizzling flesh will send a bitter prophecy   440
To Odysseus. Enough. Living, he shall go
To the House of Death and escape ocean water.
Coming home, he will find much misery.

But why do I spout forth the sorrows of Odysseus?
March, as fast as I can, and be married in Hades to my
        groom!   445
For certain that evil man shall be buried with evil rites in
        darkness,
Not by day—you who think you act great, O leader of the
        Danaans!
And I, too, a naked corpse thrown out, the gullies,
Flowing with swollen storm water near my husband's
        tomb
Will give me to beasts to eat, me the handmaid of Apollo. 450

O garlands of the most beloved of gods, sacred joys,
Good-bye. I have abandoned the festivals I once gloried in.
Go, torn from off my skin, so that being still holy in body,
I give you to be borne on swift winds for you, O mantic
        god.
Where is the general's ship? Where must I step on board? 455
No longer can you be too quick watching for a wind for
        the sails.
You shall take me out of this land as one of the three Furies.

Good-bye, mother. No tears. O beloved country
And my brothers beneath the earth and the father who
        begot us,
You shall receive me soon. I will come to the dead bringing
        victory,   460
Having ravaged the house of Atreus, which wrecked *us*.

    (CASSANDRA exits followed by TALTHYBIUS.
    HECUBA falls.)

CHORUS LEADER:
Protectors of old Hecuba, don't you see

How the queen falls speechless and prostrate?
Won't you help her? You will let an old woman
Lie there, you villains? Lift her up! 465

HECUBA:
Fallen, let me lie here. Unwanted help is not
At all welcome, my women. Falling is right
For what I suffer and have suffered and still will suffer.
O you gods! I summon evil allies,
But to call on the gods means something, 470
When one of us suffers disaster.

(HECUBA is helped up.)

So first I want to sing of joy.
That way I get more pity for my misfortunes.
I was royal, and I married royalty.
I bore the greatest children, 475
Not mere nothings, but the finest of the Phrygians,
Whom no Trojan nor Greek nor barbarian
Woman could boast of giving birth to.

I saw them fall under the Greek spear.
I cut my hair at their tombs. 480
And Father Priam—I didn't hear it from others
But saw it with my own eyes and cried—
Him butchered at the altar fire,
And the city was taken. The virgins I raised
For the honor of choice bridegrooms, 485
I had them taken from my hands, raised for others,
No hoping that they shall see me,
And I will see them no more.
And the last, the capstone of my pitiful disasters,
I go off to Greece, an old woman slave. 490

It is absolutely unbearable at my age
What they will put upon me: a doorkeeper
To guard the keys, I who bore Hector,
Or make bread and have a mat on the ground
For my wrinkled back, after a royal bedstead,   495
My flesh ragged and wrapped in rags,
The pieces of my gown, unseemly for the wealthy to
        wear.
Pathetic me, ruined because of one woman's one
        marriage:
What disasters I met with, and shall meet with!

Cassandra, my child, you who reveled with gods,   500
In what misfortunes you lost your virginity,
And you, poor Polyxena, where are you?
Neither male nor female child
Of the many I bore helps unhappy me.
So why raise me up? On what hope?   505
Lead my foot, graceful in Troy once,
A slave now, to my bed of leaves on the ground
And my stony pillow, so falling I shall perish
Wasted by tears. Do not think
Any fortunate man fortunate, until he dies.   510

CHORUS:
Sing me dirges for Troy,
Weeping and new,
O Muse, a burial hymn.
I shall now cry out in song for Troy   515
How by the four-wheeled Argive cart,
I died a wretched captive of the spear.
Greeks left that gold-studded horse that creaked to heaven
Filled with armed men   520
At the city gates.

The Trojans on
The rock called out
"Go! Ah! Our pain is gone.
Bring up the statue   525
To Zeus' Trojan daughter."
What girl did not go?
What old man from his home?
In song they found reckless
Treachery.   530

The whole race of Troy
Rushed to the gates,
Brought in the mountain pine—
A barrage of boards and death for Troy.   535
For Pallas with the divine horses.
With circling ropes of flax, like a ship,
They brought the dark hull to her temple floor,
Red with Troy's blood   540
At the goddess' seat.
When dark night came
On work and joy,
The Libyan flute rang out
And Phrygian singing.   545
The virgins raised their beating
Feet, cheerful outcries.
In homes, the radiant fires
Burnt down to black embers,
Bringing sleep.   550

With the chorus in the temple,
I was celebrating the mountain virgin,
Daughter of Zeus.
A bloody war cry across the city   555
Filled the shrines of the citadel.

Beloved newborns
Fluttered their hands
In the robes of their mothers.
Ares stepped from ambush, 560
The work of the Virgin Pallas.
The slaughter of Phrygians
Went on at the altars and
Desolate beheadings
Of husbands in their beds bore off 565
The child-bearing prizes of young women to Greece,
A sorrow for the Phrygian fatherland.

(ANDROMACHE enters with ASTYANAX, her baby,
in a wagon full of Trojan spoils.)

Hecuba, do you see Andromache here
Carried in the foreigner's wagon?
Darling Astyanax, Hector's son, 570
Is with her, close to her heaving breast.
Where are they taking you on the back of a wagon,
Poor woman,
Sitting beside Hector's bronze weapons
And the Phrygian spoils taken by the spear,
With which the son of Achilles 575
Will crown from Troy his Phthian temples?

ANDROMACHE:
Achaean lords are leading me away.

HECUBA:
No, no!

ANDROMACHE:
    Why do you sigh my song?

HECUBA:
What hell!

ANDROMACHE:
This pain!

HECUBA:
O, Zeus,

ANDROMACHE:
Misery!   580

HECUBA:
Children,

ANDROMACHE:
We were that once

HECUBA:
Our happiness is gone, and Troy is gone,

ANDROMACHE:
Accurst.

HECUBA:
My noble children gone.

ANDROMACHE:
What hell,

HECUBA:
Mine, too,

ANDROMACHE:
The pain!

HECUBA:
        Pitiful   585

ANDROMACHE:
City

HECUBA:
    That smolders still.

ANDROMACHE:
My husband, O please come,

HECUBA:
—You call my son in Hades,
Unhappy woman.—

ANDROMACHE:
Come safeguard your wife.   590

You ruiner of Greeks,

HECUBA:
My first-born child to Priam
Of all my sons then.

ANDROMACHE:
Let me lie in hell.

These are grand yearnings:

HECUBA:

      —What pains, we suffer, poor
            woman.—   595

ANDROMACHE:
A city is destroyed

HECUBA:

      —Pain lies on pain.—

ANDROMACHE:
Because of the malignant gods when your son escaped
      death,
Who destroyed the Trojan citadel for an abominable
      marriage.
Before the goddess Pallas, the bloodied bodies of the
      dead
Are stretched out for vultures to carry off. The yoke of
      slavery has reached Troy.   600

HECUBA:
O my sad country,

ANDROMACHE:

      I—weep for your abandonment.—

HECUBA:
You see the wretched end.

ANDROMACHE:

      My home where I delivered!

HECUBA:
My children, your mother in a deserted city is lost to you.
What song! What sorrow!

Tears on tears pour down   605
In our homes. The dead man forgets pain.

CHORUS:
How sweet are tears to those who have suffered
And cries of lamentation and music that has pain.

ANDROMACHE:
O mother of Hector, who wasted so many   610
Argives with his spear—You see this?

HECUBA:
I see the work of the gods: how they raise up
Things that are nothing and destroy what seems something.

ANDROMACHE:
The child and I are led away as booty. The wellborn
Inherits slavery. So great is the change.   615

HECUBA:
The power of necessity is terrifying. Cassandra
Just now was dragged away from me.

ANDROMACHE:
Oh no!
Another Ajax, it seems, has appeared,
Your daughter's second. You suffer more, too.

HECUBA:
There is neither measure nor number for my sufferings.   620
One evil competes with the next.

ANDROMACHE:
Your daughter Polyxena is dead, her throat cut
Before Achilles' tomb, a gift to a lifeless corpse.

HECUBA:

I'm cursed. That enigma Talthybius spoke
To me unclearly before is clear now.   625

ANDROMACHE:

I saw her myself. Getting down from the wagon,
I covered her corpse with garments and struck my breast.

HECUBA:

Woe on woe, child, your unholy sacrifice!
How you have died horribly!

ANDROMACHE:

Dead is dead. But her being dead   630
Is a better fortune than my being alive.

HECUBA:

My child, to die is not the same as living.
It is nothing at all. In life is hope.

ANDROMACHE:

Mother, mother of children, hear my great words,
So I may put delight in your heart.   635
I say to die is like not having been born,
And to die is better than to live in misery.
The dead no longer feel pain at all.
The fortunate man falling into misfortune
Misses in his mind his former success.   640
Polyxena, just as if she had not seen the light,
Is dead and knows nothing of her torture,
And though I hit the target of good reputation,
And won much, I missed that of good fortune.

The modest behavior that belongs to a woman   645
I produced by hard efforts in Hector's house.

First, whether the woman is at fault or not,
A bad reputation follows her
Who does not stay inside.
Putting away my desire, I remained at home.　　　　　　650
And in the house, I did not allow
The loose talk of women. Having my mind
As a good home teacher, I was satisfied.
For my husband, I had a quiet tongue
And a calm eye. I knew where I should prevail　　　　655
Over him and where he should have the victory.
That reputation reaching the Greek army
Wrecked me. When I was taken,
Achilles' son wanted me for wife.
I shall slave in the house of our murderer!　　　　　　660

If, setting aside the dear image of Hector,
I'll open my heart to my new husband,
I'll seem evil to the dead one. Or hating
The new one, I'll be hated by my master.
Though they say that one night　　　　　　　　　　　665
In a man's bed loosens a hostile woman,
I hate her who throws over
Her former husband for a new marriage
And loves another. But no horse separated
From its companion bears the yoke easy.　　　　　　670
And the savage and voiceless beast
Is without reason and inferior by nature.

But in you, O dear Hector, I had a man good for me
And great in wit and birth and wealth and courage.
You first yoked me in marriage, untouched,　　　　675
A virgin, taken from my father's house.
Now you are destroyed, and I'll be taken over the sea
To Greece, a captive under the yoke of slavery.
Does not the dead Polyxena, whom you cry for,

Have less sorrow than me? 680
For the hope that remains to all mortals
Does not go with me. Nor do I deceive myself
That I'll fare well. Still, it's sweet to think so.

CHORUS:
You, too, have come to the same disaster. Lamenting
Yours, you teach me what misery I am in. 685

HECUBA:
I myself have never been on a ship,
But I know from pictures and reports:
If a storm is moderate enough for the sailors to bear,
They have the heart to save themselves from disaster:
One at the tiller, one at the sails, 690
Another keeps out bilge. If a full sea
Churned-up overwhelms them, they let themselves
Fall to their fate in the running of the waves.
So I, having much misery,
I am voiceless and keep my tongue, 695
Such a divine wave of misery overpowers me.

But, O dear child, let go of Hector's fate.
Your tears will not save him.
Honor your new lord,
Giving the man the lure of your charm. 700
If you do this, you will please all your friends
And will raise up the son of my son
As the greatest benefit for Troy, so the sons
Of his race may establish Ilium again
And it will be a city still. 705

But from this subject, another arises.
What lackey do I see approaching,
A messenger of new resolutions?

(TALTHYBIUS enters.)

TALTHYBIUS:
Wife of Hector, once the best of the Phrygians,
Do not hate me. Unwilling I announce   710
The common message of Greeks and
          Peloponnesians.

ANDROMACHE:
What is it? Your preface is an evil beginning!

TALTHYBIUS:
It is resolved that this child. . . . How can I say it?

ANDROMACHE:
He's not to have a different master from me?

TALTHYBIUS:
No Greek will be his master.   715

ANDROMACHE:
Leave him here the last of the Trojans?

TALTHYBIUS:
I don't know how to tell you bad news easily.

ANDROMACHE:
I praise your hesitation, except in telling bad news.

TALTHYBIUS:
They shall kill your child. Now, you know the
          worst.

ANDROMACHE:
No! I hear a greater disaster than my marriage.   720

Trojan Women | 41

TALTHYBIUS:
Odysseus triumphed in the assembly . . .

ANDROMACHE:
—All the worse! I suffer beyond measure!—

TALTHYBIUS:
. . . Saying do not raise the son of the best father . . .

ANDROMACHE:
—May he win such things for his own children!—

TALTHYBIUS:
. . . That they must throw him from the Trojan towers.   725
Let this be so, and you will show yourself wiser.
Don't hold on to him. Suffer your pain nobly.
Not having strength, don't think you have power.
You are powerless. You must watch out.
City and husband are ruined. You are defeated.   730
And we are able to battle one, lone woman.
For this reason, I don't want you to desire a fight
Or to perform some shameful or hateful act
Or hurl curses at the Achaeans.
If you say anything that angers the army,   735
The child will go unburied and unpitied.
Being silent and mastering your fate,
You wouldn't leave this child's corpse without a grave,
And you yourself would make the Greeks more merciful.

ANDROMACHE:
O most beloved, O much-honored child,   740
You die at enemy hands, leaving your mother lost.
The noble birth of a father,

A safeguard for others, shall kill you.
The bravery of your father is no help to you.
O my cursed wedding bed and marriage   745
Through which I came into Hector's house,
Not to bear my son a victim for Greeks,
But a king of fruitful Asia!

O child, are you crying? Do you feel your fate?
Why grab me and hold my gown,   750
Huddling like a chick between my wings?
Hector won't come, seizing his famous spear,
Coming up out of the earth to bring your deliverance,
No father's kinsmen or Phrygian force,
But a horrible fall on your neck from on high,   755
Pitilessly breaking your breath.
O most beloved child, clasped in your mother's arms,
O sweet smell of your skin! For nothing
This breast nourished you in baby clothes.
Useless, I wore myself out, wasted with work.   760
Now, and never again, embrace your mother,
Hug her who bore you, wrap your arms
Around my back and join lips.

O Greeks, inventing barbarian crimes,
Why do you kill this blameless child?   765
O, Helen, daughter of Tyndareus, not Zeus,
I say you were born of many fathers:
First Vengeance, then Envy, Murder
And Death and as many evils as earth breeds.
I'm sure Zeus never bore you,   770
Deathbringer to many barbarians and Greeks.
May you die! With your beautiful eyes,
You shamefully destroyed the renowned plains of Troy.

Come, take him, throw him if you will.
Feast on his flesh. By the gods,   775
We are brought to nothing, and we cannot
Keep off death from my child. Veil my poor body
And throw it into the ship. A beautiful
Marriage I go to, losing my child.

CHORUS:
Poor Troy, you have lost thousands   780
For one woman and a hateful marriage.

TALTHYBIUS:
Come, boy, leaving the loving embrace
Of your tortured mother, go to the crowning
Heights of your father's towers, where,
It was decreed, to stop your breath.   785
Take him! A man must be ruthless
To herald such things
And more a friend
To heartlessness than I am.

(TALTHYBIUS takes the child and exits. The wagon
continues with ANDROMACHE.)

HECUBA:
My child, son of a cursed son,   790
We are unjustly robbed of your life,
Your mother and I. What is to become of me?
What can I do for you, unlucky child?
We can strike our heads and beat our breasts,
That we can do. My poor city!   795
Poor you! What trouble don't we have?
What stops destruction from
Rushing over us completely?

CHORUS:
O, Telamon, king of bee-breeding Salamis, you
Set your throne on the wave-encircled island   800
Opposite the blessed hill where first
Athena revealed the gray-green branch of the olive tree,
Heavenly crown and glory for gleaming Athens.
You, you came with the bow-shooter Heracles
To share great deeds,   805
Sacking Troy, *our* city,
When you arrived of old from Greece.

He led the first flower of Greeks, cheated of his horses,
And relaxed his sea oar at fair Simois,   810
Heracles, who tied the stern cables
And raised from the ship his skillful hand and
        Laomedon's
Death, and after purging the perfect stonework
Of Apollo with red blasts of flame on flame,   815
He ravaged Troy.
Twice, in two batterings,
The murderous spear smashed Trojan walls.   820

For nothing, you walk graceful by golden decanters,
Laomedon's son, Ganymede,
Who fills the cups of Zeus in glorious slavery,
While your native city is eaten by fire.   825
Salty shores
Cry out, like a bird
For her young,   830
Here for husbands, for children there,
For grandmothers there.
Your fresh bathing places,
Your schoolboy running courses are gone.
You keep your young face radiantly calm   835

With favors at the throne of Zeus,
Though Greek spears ruined
The land of Priam.   840

Eros, Eros, you came to the house of Dardanus,
The heavenly ones loving you.
How then you raised Troy high in greatness, linking
Her in wedlock to the gods. I reproach   845
Zeus no more.
The shattering light,
White-winged Dawn,
Friend to mortals, she saw Troy wrecked,   850
Saw Pergamum, too,
Though she had a husband,
A father for her children, from Troy.
A golden four-horse chariot from heaven   855
Took him above, made him the land's
Great hope. But Troy
Charms gods no more.

        (MENELAUS enters.)

MENELAUS:
O this light, shining beauty of the sun,   860
In which I shall capture my wife
Helen, for I am Menelaus,
Worn-out with labor for the Greek army.
I came to Troy, not as people think,
For a woman, but for a man who cheated   865
His host and took his wife from his home.
That man paid the penalty, thank the gods,
And he and the land fell to the Greek spear.

I have come to take the Laconian woman—it's not
    sweet
To speak the name of the wife who was mine once.   870
She is counted in this tent of captives
With the other Trojan women.
Those who fought hard for her with their spears
Gave her to me to kill or, if I wish,
To bring her back unkilled to the Argive land.   875
It seems best to me to forget Helen's fate
In Troy and take her with rapid oar
Into Greece and put her to death there,
Payment for so many friends dying at Troy.

But, go into the tent, my men,   880
Escort her out, dragging her
By her blood-soaked hair.
When fair winds blow, we shall take her to Greece.

HECUBA:
O support of earth, having your seat on earth—
Zeus, or air—whoever you are, difficult to know,   885
Either necessity of nature or mind of man,
I pray to you. In silent ways,
You lead all mortal affairs to justice.

MENELAUS:
What is this? What strange prayers you make!

HECUBA:
I praise you—if you kill your wife.   890
Avoid her sight, or she will snatch you with love.
She snares men's eyes, wipes out cities,

Burns homes. She has such magic.
I know her. You do, too, and those who have suffered.

(HELEN enters, finely dressed.)

HELEN:
Menelaus, This is a fearful start.   895
I am brought out before the tent
In the hands of your servants by force.
I suppose you hate me. All the same,
I wish to ask what decision
Have the Greeks and you made on my life?   900

MENELAUS:
Nothing definite, but the whole army
Gave you to me, the man you cheated, to kill.

HELEN:
Then can I speak to this decision,
Showing that if I die, I die unjustly?

MENELAUS:
I came not for words, but to kill you.   905

HECUBA:
Hear her! Do not kill her without this,
Menelaus, and let me answer her.
You know nothing of the trouble
In Troy. The whole argument together
Will kill her. There is no escape.   910

MENELAUS:
This takes time. Still if she wishes to speak,
Let her. But know I grant it
On account of your words, not for her sake.

HELEN:
Whether I speak well or badly, you probably
Will not answer, considering me an enemy.   915
And I, against what I think you will charge me with,
I shall answer, opposing
My accusations to yours.

First, this woman bore the beginning of trouble
By giving birth to Paris, and, second, the old man   920
Destroyed Troy and me by not killing the baby,
The painful image of a firebrand, then called Alexander.

Hear the rest of what happened.
He judged this triple group of goddesses.
The gift of Athena to Alexander was to destroy   925
Greece by commanding a Trojan army.
Hera held out rule over Asia
And the boundaries of Europe, if she won.
Aphrodite, wondering at my looks,
Offered me, if she surpassed the goddesses   930
In beauty. Consider what followed next.
Aphrodite won. My marriage blessed Greece,
So it is not ruled by barbarians,
Neither through spear nor tyranny.
Greece prospered by what destroyed me.   935
Sold for my beauty, I am blamed
By those who should crown my head.

You will say I have not spoken to the point:
How I left your house secretly.
Having no minor goddess with him,   940
This demon of Hecuba, call him
Alexander or Paris, as you wish,
This man, you worst of husbands, you left
In your home and sailed from Sparta to Crete.

Now.
I shall question, not you, but myself: 945
What was I thinking, going off from my house
With a stranger, giving up country and home?
Punish the goddess, if you are stronger than Zeus,
Who has power over the other gods,
Though he is Love's slave. So forgive me.   950

But you may raise a false objection against me.
After Alexander died and went deep under earth,
Because my god-prepared marriage was no more,
I should have left my house and gone to the Greek
    ships.
I tried this very thing. The tower keepers   955
And the guards on the walls are my witnesses,
Who often discovered me secretly letting myself
Down from the battlements to the ground on a rope.

Deiphobus, that new husband, took me
And held me as wife against the will of the Trojans.   960
How could I die legitimately, my husband,
And justly and by you, I who married by force,
My domestic life bitter slavery, instead
Of a reward for victory. If you want power
Over gods, your desire is mindless.   965

CHORUS:
My queen, protect your children and country,
Break her eloquence, because she speaks well,
And does wrong—a terrible thing.

HECUBA:
I shall become the ally of the goddesses
And show she spoke unjustly.   970
I don't think Hera and the virgin goddess

Reached such heights of stupidity
That Hera would sell Argos to barbarians,
Or Pallas ever sell Athens in slavery to Troy.
They did not come to Ida for such childish games   975
And pride in their looks. Did the goddess
Hera have such love of beauty,
So she could get a husband better than Zeus?
Or Athena hunting for a marriage with some god,
She who begged her father for virginity   980
And fled marriage? Don't make the goddesses silly
To gloss over your crimes. You won't convince the wise.

You said Aphrodite—which is ridiculous—
Came with my son to Menelaus' house.
Could she not have remained calmly in heaven   985
And brought you and the whole city of Amyclae to Troy?

It was my most remarkably handsome son,
And, seeing him, your mind became Aphrodite.
All such stupidity is Aphrodite to mortals. For truly
Does the goddess' name begin like *aphrodisiac*.   990
Seeing him shining in barbarian dress
And gold, you went stark mad.
You were raised frugally in Argos.
Freed from Sparta, you hoped to flood
Troy, already awash with gold, with your extravagance.   995
The home of Menelaus was not enough
For you to riot in your luxury.

Well then.
You say my son took you by force.
What Spartan saw you? What outcry
Did you make, young Castor and his brother   1000
Still being alive and not yet among the stars?
After you came to Troy, the Argives

On your trail, the battle was to the death.
If this man's actions were reported better,
You praised Menelaus, so that my son   1005
Suffered, having a great rival in love.
If the Trojans prospered, this man was nothing.
Watching fortune, you worked it so that
You followed her and chose not to follow virtue.
Then you say you secretly let yourself down   1010
From the walls by a rope, as if kept against your will.

Where were you caught hanging by a noose
Or sharpening a sword, which a high-born woman
Would do, longing for her ex-husband?
I advised you many, many times: 1015
"My daughter, go home! My child will make
Another marriage. I shall send you to the Achaean
        ships,
Helping you sneak away. Stop the war
Between the Greeks and us!" You hated this.

You ran rampant in Alexander's palace and wanted   1020
Barbarians to prostrate themselves before you.
This meant something to you. And *now*
You come decked out, seeing the same sky
As your husband, you despicable bitch.
You should have come humble in rags,   1025
Wracked with fear, head shorn,
Showing shame rather than shamelessness
For the crimes you have committed.

Menelaus, know my conclusion:
Crown Greece by nobly killing this woman,   1030
And set the law for others:
Whoever betrays her husband, dies.

CHORUS:
Menelaus, take a vengeance on your wife worthy
Of your ancestors and home. Avoid unmanly blame
In Greece. Be noble before your enemies.   1035

MENELAUS:
You agree with me in this matter:
That she went from my home of her own free will
To a foreign bed. Aphrodite was brought into her story
So she could brag. Go to the stone-throwers!
Pay quickly for the long suffering of the Achaeans   1040
With death and learn not to disgrace me!

HELEN:
No, I grab your knees! Don't kill me,
Blaming me for the madness of the goddesses! Forgive!

HECUBA:
Don't betray your allies she has already killed.
I beg you on their behalf and their children.   1045

MENELAUS:
Stop, old woman. I take no thought of her.
I'm telling my servants to take her
To the ships, from there to be taken to sea.

HECUBA:
Don't let her go in the same ship as you.

MENELAUS:
What? Has she put on weight?   1050

HECUBA:
There is no lover who does not always love.

MENELAUS:
The minds of lovers vary.
But let it be as you wish. She shall not
Go in the same ship. You speak well.
Reaching Argos, this rotten wife will die   1055
The painful death she deserves and will instill
Chastity in all women. This is not easy.
Nevertheless, her destruction will strike fear
Into their stupidity, even if they are more hateful than
          her.

(MENELAUS exits with HELEN.)

CHORUS:
Could you betray the temples   1060
In Ilium to the Achaeans
So easily, and altars of sweet incense,
O Zeus, and flame of honeyed offerings,
The smoke of heavenly myrrh,
Blest Pergamum, and Ida's, Ida's   1065
Ravines of ivy wreaths that run
With rivers of the melted snow,
The boundary struck first by the dawn,
The sacred dwelling lit by sunlight?   1070

Gone are the sacrifices,
The holy music of the choirs,
And all-night vigils for the gods in darkness,
The statues with their profiles of gold,
And festivals of the moon   1075
In Phrygia that number twelve.
I worry, Lord, if you care for
These things upon your heavenly throne:

The burning of the ruined city,
Attacked by fire and blasted apart.   1080

Husband, dear husband,
Dead, you wander about,
Unburied, unclean, while a sea-ship   1085
Fluttering its wings ravishes me away
To grazing Argos, where the people live
Within Cyclopean walls sky-high.
At the gates, a multitude of our children
Cling and cry and cry and cry,   1090
"Mother, no, please no, the Achaeans pull me
Away, alone, without you,
From your sight to their dark ship
With sea-oars to   1095
Sacred Salamis,
Or the Isthmian headland, open
Two ways, where Pelops' palace
Guards the Peloponnesus."

Flashing with lightning,   1100
May Aegean's blest fire
Hurled with all might strike amidships
Menelaus' oars in mid-sea, since he
Sends me away in tears, in tears from Troy,   1105
A slave from home to Hellas while
Helen, Zeus' daughter, happens to hold
Golden mirrors, the joy of girls.
May he not come to the Laconian land,   1110
His fatherland and his hearth
Nor the city of Pitane
And its bronze-gated
Temple, capturing

His cheating wife, great Greece's shame,   1115
That brought such miserable suffering
To the river Simois.

Oh, no!
New misfortunes follow new misfortunes
In our land. Look, unhappy wives of Troy,
At this corpse of Astyanax,   1120
Some discus horribly flung from the towers.
Greeks have killed him.

(TALTHYBIUS enters with the corpse of ASTYANAX.)

TALTHYBIUS:
Hecuba, one last oared ship is about
To carry by sea the remaining spoils
Of Achilles' son to the coast of Phthia.   1125
Neoptolemus himself has set sail,
Hearing some bad news of his grandfather.
Acastus, Pelias' son, has driven him from the country.
So he went quickly. He didn't have the luxury
Of delay. Andromache is with him,   1130
Bringing me to many tears as she left,
Moaning for her fatherland and saying farewell
To Hector's tomb. She asked Neoptolemus
To bury this child, who, hurled from the walls,
Breathed out his life, the son of your Hector.   1135

And this bronze-backed shield, the terror of Achaeans,
This, that his father threw over his ribs,
She asked him not to take it to Peleus' hearth
Nor into the room where she will be bedded,
For Andromache, the dead child's mother,   1140
A painful sight. But to bury the boy in the shield

Instead of cedar wood or surrounding stone,
To give him into your arms to wrap the corpse
With robes and wreaths as best as you can,
Since she is gone and her master's haste   1145
Would not let her bury her own child.

We, when you have dressed the body,
Will cover it in earth and take to sea.
Do your duty as fast as possible.
I saved you one torture.   1150
Crossing Scamander's streams,
I washed the body and cleansed its wounds.
But now I go to break ground for the grave,
And cut short the work you and I must do
To set our ship on course for home.   1155

HECUBA:
Put the fine-rounded shield on the ground,
A sad spectacle, unwelcome in my sight.

(TALTHYBIUS exits.)

Why, O Achaeans, did you fear this young child,
Prouder of your spear than your brain,
And commit such outrageous murder? Would he stand   1160
Fallen Troy up again someday? How empty you are!
Though Hector triumphed with his spear
With thousands of others, we still perished.
But when the city died and the Phrygians were ruined,
You feared this tiny baby. I do not honor fear   1165
In one who fears and does not think.

O dearest, what a misfortune your death is!
If you died for the city, reaching manhood,

Marriage, and the godlike kingship, you would have
       been blessed
—If any of these things are blessed. But now, unaware,   1170
Neither seeing nor knowing these things,
Child, you experienced nothing of your inheritance.
Unlucky you, your country's walls,
Towered by Apollo, horribly gashed the curls
Your mother bore and cultivated so much   1175
And covered with kisses, where blood laughs out
Among broken bones—how shamelessly I speak!

O hands, how you are the sweet images
Of your father's, but lie loose in the sockets.
O dear mouth, promising much, you are ruined   1180
And have deceived me, burying yourself in my gown,
Saying, "O grandmother, I shall cut a great lock
Of curls off for you and bring groups of my friends
To your grave and give a loving eulogy." Now you
Don't bury me, but I you, a sorry, younger corpse,   1185
Me an old, cityless, childless woman.
O, the many hugs, the nursery care,
The naps we shared, all gone.
What could a poet write upon your grave?
"The Achaeans killed this child from fear"?   1190
The inscription is disgraceful to Greece.
Not having your inheritance, you shall have
Instead a bronze-backed shield for a tomb.

O shield, that saved the beautiful arm
Of Hector, you have lost your best guardian.   1195
How sweet the impression lies in the handle,
and in the circular rim of the shield
The sweat, which long-struggling Hector dropped
From his forehead and left from his beard.

Go, bring in ornament for the sad corpse,   1200
Whatever you can. Fate leaves
No glamour here. What I have, you shall get.
That mortal is a fool who seems successful
And always rejoices. Fate in its ways,
Like a crazy man, leaps here and there.   1205
The same man is never happy forever.

CHORUS:
Here at hand, the women are bringing you ornaments
From the Phrygian spoils to deck your dead body.

HECUBA:
O child, your father's mother places on you,
Not prizes, won with horses or bows over your friends, 1210
Customs Phrygians honor in moderation,
But gifts once your own. Helen, hated by the gods,
Took everything, took you, and killed your life
And wrecked totally our whole royal house.   1215

CHORUS:
There, there, you strike,
You strike my heart, my once great lord
Of the city!

HECUBA:
Glorious Phrygian robes that should have dressed
Your body in marriage to the highest Asian princess,
I put on your flesh. And you, beloved shield   1220
Of Hector, once the mother of countless
Trophies, receive this crown.
Dying with the dead, you do not die.
Since it is better by far to honor you
Than the weapons of clever, cowardly Odysseus.   1225

CHORUS:
Gods! Gods!
The land weeps bitterly
To receive you, my child.
Weep, mother

HECUBA:
—O gods!—

CHORUS:
A lament of the dead.

HECUBA:

What now!   1230

CHORUS:
O gods, indeed, your unforgettable pain!

HECUBA:
I shall heal your wounds with bandages,
A pathetic doctor in name, but powerless.
Your father will tend you among the dead.

CHORUS:
Strike, strike your head!   1235
Blows of the hand, like oars!
Me! What pain!

HECUBA:
Most beloved women!

CHORUS:
Hecuba, tell us. What are you crying?

HECUBA:
The gods care about nothing except my pain   1240
And Troy hated beyond other cities.
We slaughtered oxen for nothing. But had not a god
Overturned the land and thrown down what stood up,
We would be unknown and not hymned by the muses,
Providing songs for men to come.   1245

Go, bury the corpse in its pitiful grave.
He has the death cloths he needs.
I think it matters little to the dead,
If someone is buried in rich clothes.
That is an empty boast of the living.   1250

(The corpse of ASTYANAX is carried out.)

CHORUS:
Pure hell!
Poor mother, her great hopes
For your life mangled!
Child, greatly happy, descended
From noble ancestors,
Destroyed by terrible death.   1255

What more!
Who do I see on top of Troy,
Waving hands flaming

With torches? Some new disaster
Is about to fall on Troy.

(TALTHYBIUS enters.)

TALTHYBIUS:
I call you captains who were ordered   1260
To burn this city of Priam. No longer
Keep the flame idle in your hand but hurl fire,
So we may level the city of Priam
And set out happily from Troy.

This order is double: 1265
When the chiefs sound the shrill blast
Of the trumpet, move ahead, daughters of Troy,
To the Achaean ships and so depart the land.

You, most wretched old woman, follow them!
These men come after you from Odysseus,   1270
Whose allotment takes you a slave from your homeland.

HECUBA:
Cursed me. This is the last
And end of all my sufferings.
I leave my country. My city flares upward.
But, old foot, hurry as you can,   1275
So I may say good-bye to the dying city. O grand city,
Once proud in spirit among the barbarians,
How quick you will lose your glorious name.
They burn you, leading us as slaves from the land.

O, gods! But why do I call on the gods?   1280
Called before, they did not listen.

Come, let me rush into the funeral pyre!
How very beautiful for me to die with the blazing
      fatherland!

(HECUBA rushes at the flames, but TALTHYBIUS drags
her back.)

TALTHYBIUS:
You are possessed, poor thing,
Because of your troubles. Come, men! No delay.   1285
You must hand to Odysseus this woman, his prize.

HECUBA:
Gods, gods, gods!
Son of Cronus, Phrygian Lord, Ancestor,
Father, do you see what things unworthy
Of your race we suffer?   1290

CHORUS:
He sees. The great city—
Now no city—is ruined. Troy is no longer.

HECUBA:
Gods, gods, gods!
Ilium blazes. The buildings   1295
Of the citadel burn down
And the city and the tops of the walls.

CHORUS:
Like smoke on a heavenly wing,
Our land, fallen to the spear, crumbles away.
Houses are overrun with furious fire   1300
And the killing spear.

HECUBA:
O country, nurse of my children!

CHORUS:
Why! Why!

HECUBA:
My children hear, and know your mother's voice!

CHORUS:
With your lament you call upon the dead!

HECUBA:
Putting my old limbs upon the ground,   1305
I make it ring with my two fists.

CHORUS:
I follow you and set my knee
On earth and call my suffering husband
Below.

HECUBA:
We are led, we are taken

CHORUS:
             —You cry pain, pain!—   1310

HECUBA:
Under a roof for a slave,

CHORUS:
             Far from my home.

HECUBA:
O Priam, O Priam,
You are ruined, graveless, friendless,
Blind to my misfortune.

CHORUS:
Black death has covered his eyes: 1315
Holy, and unholy, slaughter.

HECUBA:
O temples, beloved city

CHORUS:
Why! Why!

HECUBA:
You own the murderous fire and spearhead's point.

CHORUS:
You shall fall quick and nameless on dear soil.

HECUBA:
Dust like a smoky wing to heaven   1320
Will make my home invisible.

CHORUS:
The name of Troy shall disappear.
One thing gone here, another there.
Troy's gone.

HECUBA:
Notice that? Did you hear?

CHORUS:

                             Yes, the towers crash.   1325

HECUBA:
Earthquake, an earthquake, the whole

CHORUS:

                                  City it swamps.

HECUBA:
No, no! O my trembling,
Trembling limbs, make my feet move!
Go to days of slave-life.   1330

CHORUS:
Poor city! Nevertheless—
March to the Achaean ships!

       (The trumpet sounds. TALTHYBIUS exits followed by
       HECUBA and the Trojan women.)

Notes

1–52. Prologue (what precedes the introduction of the chorus. Aristotle, *Poetics*, 1452b19–20). A frame scene and a divine perspective on the action (1–97). (See the introduction.) Followed by Hecuba's song (98–153).

1. *Poseidon.* King Laomedon of Troy cheated Poseidon of his wages after he built a sea wall at Troy, so Poseidon remained an enemy of the Trojans during the Trojan War (*Iliad* 21.441–460). Poseidon is sympathetic to them in this play and intensifies our sympathies by emphasizing the excessive violence of the Greeks.

2. *Nereids.* Sea-goddesses.

7. *Phrygians* are the same as Trojans.

9. *Achaean* = Greek. *Parnassus*. Phocis is an area of northern Greece where the Mount Parnassus range is located.

13–14. These lines are thought to be an interpolation by an actor.

16–17. Poseidon cites the atrocity of King Priam of Troy being murdered at the sacred hearth that should have been a sanctuary, protected by Zeus *Herkeios* ("Of the Household"). Poseidon had helped build the sanctuary. For the killing of Priam by Achilles' son, Neoptolemus, see Virgil, *Aeneid* 2.526–558.

23. *Argive* = Greek. *Hera*. Queen of the gods.

28. *Scamander*. A river near Troy.

30. Arcadia, in the south, and Thessaly, in the north, are sections of Greece. *Theseus* was a great hero and a legendary king of Athens.

40. *Achilles*. Greek hero at Troy.

42. Apollo gave Cassandra the gift of prophecy, but she rejected his sexual advances. Unable to take his gift back, he gave her the curse of never being believed. Her virginity was sacred to Apollo.

43. *Agamemnon*. Leader of the Greek forces.

49. Poseidon is the brother of Zeus.

65–66. Athena's decision to punish the Greeks frames the action of the tragedy, adding to the sympathy for the Trojans and condemning Greek crimes.

69–70. The Greek *Ajax*, son of Oileus, raped Cassandra in Athena's temple. Cf. note to 42.

84. *Euboea*. Large island near Athens.

89–90. *Myconos, Delos, Scyros,* and *Lemnos* are Aegean islands. *Caphareus* is an eastern promontory of the island of Euboea.

98–152. Hecuba's song (monody). In contrast to the formal, divine dialogue of Poseidon and Athena, Hecuba's grief is augmented by her astrophic lyric measures (sung).

132. *Castor* was a brother of Helen.

153–229. Parodos. The introductory ode of the chorus. 153–175: Strophe A. 176–196: Antistrophe A. 197–213: Strophe B. 214–229: Antistrophe B. 153–196 is a *kommós*, a lament between Hecuba and the chorus, emphasizing their bonding in misery. Unlike Hecuba, the chorus speculates on where they may go as slaves, suggesting life after Troy. Longing for, and invoking, faraway places is characteristic of Euripidean choruses (e.g., *Bacchae*, 402–416).

168–169. Hecuba thinks of her possessed daughter as a *maenad*, or follower of Dionysos (Bacchus).

184. *Danaan* = Greek.

188. Phthia is in northern Greece.

206. Pirene is a spring in Corinth.

210. The *Eurotas* is a river in Sparta.

216. The *Peneus* is a river in northern Greece.

220–221. Etna is the volcano in Sicily where the smith god, Hephaestus, had his forge.

223. *Carthage*. A city in north Africa.

225–226. The *Ionian* Sea is between Greece and Italy where the river *Crathis* is. Greeks inhabited Italy at this time.

230–510. First Episode. Introductory Greek anapests (230–234). Hecuba's lament (278–292). Cassandra's song (308–341). 308–324: Strophe. 325–341: Antistrophe. Cassandra's recitative (Greek trochaic tetrameters) (444–461).

234. *Dorian*. Southern Greece, standing for Greece in general here.

243. Cadmus founded the Greek city of Thebes.

250–251. *the Laconian / Lady* is Clytemnestra, wife of Agamemnon and sister of Helen.

274. *Achilles' son*. Neoptolemus.

278–292. Hecuba's violent reaction shifts her dialogue to lyric. Odysseus, though a hero in the *Odyssey*, is often a villain (e.g., in Sophocles' *Philoctetes*).

301. *Argos*. A city near Sparta.

308–341. Cassandra's wild song mixes iambic, dochmiac ($\smile$— — $\smile$—), and aeolic (basically choriambic, — $\smile\smile$—) verses. She blends death song and marriage song (cf. *Hecuba*, 209–210). Then she changes key to "outside my bacchic madness" and prophesies truly in dialogue measures but is fated never to be believed.

310. *Hymen*. God of marriage.

320. As mother of the bride, Hecuba was supposed to hold the bridal torch.

323. *Hecate*. A goddess of the underworld.

326. *Evoe*. The traditional bacchic cry.

327. *Phoebus* = Apollo.

343. *Hephaestus*. See note to 220–221.

370. Agamemnon sacrificed his daughter Iphigenia to make the winds blow for the expedition to Troy.

372. *for his brother*. Agamemnon's brother is Menelaus, husband of Helen.

374. *Scamander's banks*. See note to 28.

376. *Ares*. God of War.

398. Zeus' daughter. Helen was reputedly the daughter of Zeus, who, in the shape of a swan, raped her mother, Leda.

421. *son of Laertes*. Odysseus.

425–430. On the fate of Hecuba, see the introduction.

435–443. [*Beyond*]. Some words are missing from the manuscripts. *Charybdis, Cyclops*, and *Circe* are two monsters and a witch confronted by Odysseus. See Homer's *Odyssey* (books 9–12) for all the events in this passage.

447. *leader of the Danaans*. Agamemnon.

457. *the three Furies*. Erinyes, inexorable goddesses of vengeance from the underworld.

444–462. Greek trochaic tetrameters (eight trochees to a line) extend the line, making Cassandra's prophesy more formal, while the falling rhythm forecasts more tragedy to come after the action of the play, including her own murder.

509–510. *Do not think / Any fortunate man fortunate until he dies*. A Greek commonplace originally attributed to Solon the Lawgiver (Herodotus 1.32).

511–567. First Stasimon (Choral Ode). 511–530: Strophe. 531–550: Antistrophe. 551–567: Epode.

526. *Zeus' daughter*. Athena.

568–798. Second Episode. Introductory anapests (568–576.) Andromache and Hecuba Duet (557–607). 577–581: Strophe A. 582–586: Antistrophe A. 587–590: Strophe B. 591–594: Antistrophe B. 595–607: Epode. A vivid and personal re-creation of the fall of Troy (cf. Virgil, *Aeneid* 2), which prepares for the introduction of another victim of the war, Andromache, wife of Hector. Note that the *antilabé*, or split lines, add to the lyric intensity, as Hecuba and Andromache lament mainly their own individual fates till the fate of Astyanax brings them together.

597. *your son*. Alexander, or Paris. This story was the subject of the first play in the trilogy, *Alexandros*. See the introduction.

704. *Ilium* = Troy.

711. *Peloponnesians*. Southern Greeks.

725. Odysseus' murder of Astyanax is mentioned in the *Sack of Troy* of the Epic Cycle (7–6 C).

782–798. Greek exit anapests.

799–859. Second Choral Ode. "The Telamon Ode" (or "The Ganymede Ode"). 799–808: Strophe A. 809–819: Antistrophe A. 820–839: Strophe B. 840–859: Antistrophe B. The chorus' despair leads to their recalling the cursed history of Troy: How Telamon and Heracles destroyed Troy before the Greeks did. Then they lament the divine friends of Troy who failed to protect the city.

799–816. *Telamon.* Uncle of Achilles. Telamon helped Heracles destroy Troy earlier. *Salamis.* An island near Athens and traditionally the home of Euripides.

809. *cheated of his horses.* Heracles had rescued Hesione, daughter of King Laomedon of Troy. Laomedon promised Heracles wonderful horses that he had received from Zeus, but he never gave them to him. Laomedon was the father of Priam. Notice the many references to treachery in the play (1, 9–12, etc.).

810. *Simois.* A river near Troy.

821. *Ganymede.* Zeus carried off the Trojan boy, Ganymede, to be his cupbearer and lover.

840–856. *Eros.* God of love. Eros inflamed Zeus with love for Ganymede and the goddess of Dawn (Eos) with love for the Trojan Tithonus, thus connecting the gods and Troy. *Dardanus.* A son of Zeus, he was the founder of Troy.

851. *Pergamum.* The citadel of Troy.

860–1059. Third Episode. A shift in the action to a "trial" scene about the cause of the Trojan War. Menelaus now enters, not the great hero in Homer's *Iliad* but the famed cuckold who now engages in a power struggle with his runaway wife (cf. *Odyssey*, 4.137–289).

869. *Laconian.* Spartan.

884–888. Hecuba reflects some Sophist speculation of the time. Anaximenes thought that air was the basic substance and determined the world, as soul determined the body. Soul itself was air. Anaxagoras posited *nous*, or mind. Doubts about the tales of the gods are common in Euripides (e.g., *Helen*, 1138–1142) and show the increasing rationalism of the age. But we must realize the dramatic context in which such speculations occur. Here we see into the contradictory mind of a tormented woman who feels abandoned by the traditional gods and divine justice she has always believed in; yet she needs to believe. Euripides was a friend of the Sophists and influenced by them.

914–965. Helen speaks a set speech (*rhesis*), reminiscent of law courts. Hecuba answers her with another (969–1032). Greek tragedy and Greek oratory are nearly allied. Helen's speech has similarities with two prose defenses of Helen: Gorgias' *Encomium of Helen* (undatable) and Isocrates' *Encomium to Helen* (date uncertain but later than this play). The first defends Helen as victim (see the introduction). The second sees Helen as protecting Greece from Trojan domination, as she claims here (932–937).

920. *the old man*. Priam. See the introduction for the *Alexandros*, the first play in the trilogy. Alexander, "defender of men," is another name for Paris. In that play, Hecuba dreams that she gave birth to a stick of burning wood (the *firebrand* of line 922).

959. *Deiphobus*, brother of Paris and Hector, who later married Helen at Troy. He was killed and mangled by Menelaus.

973. *Argos*. See note to 301.

975. *Ida*. A mountain range near Troy.

986. *Amyclae*. A city near Sparta.

988–990. *Aphrodite/aphrodisiac*. The pun in Greek is not possible to reproduce in English: Aphrodite ("Love") begins like *aphrosyne* ("mindlessness").

1000. *Castor and his brother*. Castor and Pollux, brothers of Helen, now the constellation Gemini. Cf. line 132.

1060–1117. Third Choral Ode. 1060–1070: Strophe A. 1071–1080: Antistrophe A. 1081–1099: Strophe B. 1100–1117: Antistophe B. The chorus now blames Zeus himself for not helping their city, whose natural beauty and glorious festivals are now gone, and personalizes the tragedy by prophesying the future, and finally curses Menelaus' return.

1066. *Ida's*. A local story claimed that the mountain, the boundary of ocean and land, gathered rays of light from the sea and made them into the rising sun.

1088. *Cyclopean*. The Cyclopes are cannibalistic giants. See notes to 435–443.

1097. *Salamis*. See note to 799.

1098–1099. *Isthmian*. The Isthmus of Corinth forms the entrance to the Peloponnesus, "Pelops' Island," or southern Greece. Cf. line 711.

1110. *Laconian*. See line 869.

1112. *Pitane*. A section of Sparta.

1114. *Temple*. Of Athena.

1117. *Simois*. See line 810.

1118–1332. Exodos. Transitional Greek anapests (1118–1122). From 1216 to the end the verse becomes lyric, except for Talthybius' order to burn down the citadel (the houses were burning at the beginning of the play), Hecuba's reaction, and his order for the women to leave (1260–1286). 1302–1316: Strophe. 1317–1332: Antistrophe.

1125. *Phthia*. See line 188.

1128. *Acastus*. King of Iolcos; befriended Peleus, grandfather of Neoptolemus and father of Achilles. According to this passage, Acastus later drove Peleus out of Iolcos.

1152. *Scamander's streams*. See line 28.

1288. *Son of Cronus*. Zeus. Dardanus, founder of Troy, was a son of Zeus. Cf. note to 840.

1316. *Holy, and unholy, slaughter*. Priam was killed at the altar of Zeus. Cf. lines 16–17.

HELEN

Introduction

At the center of Greek—and Roman—myth was the Trojan War, and at the center of the Trojan War was its cause, Helen, Zeus' daughter, supposedly abducted from Sparta by Paris to Troy. Helen of Troy remains central to Greek mythology, even today. If ancient Greek society was in many ways male-dominated, the power and volatility of women created its myths, whether the women were goddesses like Hera, Athena, and Persephone, or aristocratic women like Antigone, Clytemnestra, and Penelope. Interpretations of Helen's story are found from Homer to Marlowe to Goethe to the modern poet H.D., and beyond. She embodies that quintessential Greek pursuit, beauty. Aeschylus punned on her name in the *Agamemnon* (688–690) and may have used a popular etymology, likening her name to a word meaning "to take, capture, destroy," suggesting her predatory powers (Skutsch, "Helen"). Her name can also mean a "torch" in Greek. She was probably a nature goddess, like Persephone, whose abductions (by Theseus as well as Paris) represent changes in the seasons. She became a patron deity of girls' coming to sexual maturity and marriage, and a cult figure. In literature, she often represents desire and destruction.

In her early legend, she is offered by Aphrodite as a prize in the beauty contest on Mount Ida, a bribe for Paris to choose her as the most beautiful goddess over Hera and Athena, both of whom offer the conquest of Greece. Menelaus, her husband, and Agamemnon, his brother, muster the Greeks to bring her back. After a ten-year siege, Troy falls to the wooden-horse stratagem of Odysseus, and Helen returns safely to Sparta. Helen's inner life is the key to variations of the story: Did she run off with Paris or was she dragged? Was she whore or victim? In the *Odyssey*, she laments her Trojan adventure and says she longed for home. Menelaus scoffs at her tale (4.235–289).

But she has an alternative tale. In the *Cypria* of the Epic Cycle (7–6 C.), Helen is a victim of the "plan of Zeus" to rid the earth of its excess population. To Gorgias, in the seemingly light-hearted *Encomium of Helen*, she is not to blame but is the victim of four powerful forces: the gods (or chance), force, rhetoric, and love. Sappho celebrates Helen leaving all for love (Fragment 16). Stesichorus goes even further. He claims that after he attacked Helen in a poem he was struck blind, and then wrote a retraction that stated she never went to Troy at all but was in Egypt during the war, for which Helen restored his sight. The historian Herodotus, too, insists that Helen was in Egypt after being blown off course for Troy with Paris. Proteus, king of Egypt, took Helen away from her abductor, and Paris continued on to Troy and fought the war for a lie (2.112–120).

Euripides likely knew these sources and others that have been lost. Apollo reveals Zeus' plan in Euripides' *Orestes*:

. . . the gods, because of her great beauty,
Set Greeks and Trojans against one another
And brought death, so they might lighten the outrage
Of the plentiful surplus of men from the earth. (1639–1642)

In *Electra*, Euripides mentions Helen's sojourn in Egypt. Castor, brother of Helen, is speaking:

From the palace of Proteus,
len came, leaving Egypt and did not go to Troy.
so there might be strife and murder of men,
t a phantom there. (1280–1283)

the heroine herself proclaims the plan of Zeus to
of men and to raise up Achilles as the greatest
ge:

Zeus' plans fit well with this misery:
He brought a Greek war to the land
And to the poor Trojans, so he might lighten
Mother Earth of crowds of mortals and make
Known the mightiest man in Greece. (37–41)

Helen was performed in Athens in 412 BC. Then the mode was to rework older heroic tales of Troy and the royal House of Thebes. But (from what we can tell) Euripides went beyond his sources that helped form what a character in Aristophanes called "the new Helen" of Euripides (*Women at the Thesmophoria*, 950). In our play, Helen is the still chaste wife of Menelaus, taken to Egypt by Hermes so she would not be bedded by Paris at all. In Egypt, Proteus' son, Theoclymenus, pursues her, while she claims sanctuary in the tomb of the now-dead Proteus. Helen has become Penelope, traditionally her opposite.

Greek tragedy in Aristotle's definition needs to arouse pity and fear (1451b) but need not have a tragic ending (1452b), as in Euripides' *Iphigenia in Tauris*. The tragic style of *Helen* is more relaxed than usual, even humorous in places. Ancient and modern critics have noted that Euripides' style in general is more colloquial than the styles of Aeschylus and Sophocles, and P. T. Stevens (*Colloquial Expressions*, 65) discovered forty-nine colloquial expressions in this play, a high percentage for even Euripidean Greek tragedy. Menelaus in disguise discusses his own funeral, and he and Helen sometimes employ double entendres, taking advantage of that situational irony (e.g., 1287–1300). The play's themes of exoticism, mistaken identity, disguise, connivance, recognition, reunion, and hairbreadth escapes are common in later literature, but their use here i different. What distinguishes *Helen* from later "tragicomed and "romantic tragedies" is its seriousness and its air of menace, in spite of its comic moments. As we saw above, H is again the victim of the will of Zeus, and she laments th of human life at Troy in her name, where soldiers die for a phantom. Like a Homeric hero, Helen is pained at her bad and unearned reputation and connives like Odysseus to escape from her tragic life in Egypt. Frustrated and inept, Menelaus takes a secondary role. Helen shows what complex situations female intelligence can resolve and demonstrates to the Athenian audience the female intellect they have ignored. When battle breaks out, Menelaus resumes his heroic Homeric role, and Helen drives him on. This battle is as right as the Trojan War was wrong. Ultimately, war was Zeus' mysterious will, whatever his plan. Moreover, the play examines the conflict between illusion and reality, the senses and truth, myth and identity.

The Egyptians are partly "Hellenized." Although an Egyptian, Theoclymenus acts the familiar Greek tragic tyrant, while his sister exemplifies Greek piety and reason, another example of the wisdom of Euripides' women. Heroically, she risks her life for Helen and Menelaus. The Greeks admired Egypt, borrowed from it, and felt superior to it—and to everyone else non-Greek. So in this play Egyptians are also "barbarians." Such complexity permeates the plot and dialogue.

Central to the extensive imagery of the play is flying. Hermes took Helen by air to Egypt, stopping at what is now Makronissos, to name the island Helen after her. The eidolon, the phantom Helen that deceives Menelaus and accompanies him to Troy and then to Egypt, miraculously flies off. Finally the Dioscuri, Castor and Polydeuces, ride down their track of air on the crane over the stage. Castor announces they will fly over the sea to guide Helen and Menelaus home. The images of flying create a sense of wonder and awe. Flying stresses the power of the gods and the mystery of the world—and Helen's favored status. From the sky, Castor proclaims Helen's coming apotheosis. The daughter of Zeus will be rewarded for her pains by being celebrated and worshipped forever. But in this play, she is very human indeed.

Note on the Greek Text

In general, I have followed James Diggle's Oxford Classical Text, *Euripides Fabulae*, III (1994). (Line numbering corresponds to Diggle's text, not to my translation.) I have also used the following editions:

G. Murray, Euripides, *Euridipidis Fabulae*, III (Oxford: Oxford University Press, 1913).
A. M. Dale, Euripides, *Helen* (Oxford: Clarendon Press, 1967), with commentary.
R. Kannicht, Euripides, *Helena*, 2 vols. (Heidelberg: Winter, 1969), with commentary.
D. Kovacs, Euripides, V, *Helen, Phoenician Women, Orestes* (Cambridge, MA: Harvard University Press, 2002).
W. Allan, Euripides, *Helen* (Cambridge: Cambridge University Press, 2008), with commentary.

List of Characters

HELEN OF TROY
TEUCER, Greek soldier
CHORUS of Greek Women
MENELAUS, Helen's husband
OLD WOMAN, Theoclymenus' servant
SERVANT of Menelaus
THEONOE ("Theono-e"), Theoclymenus' sister
THEOCLYMENUS, King of Egypt
MESSENGER, an Egyptian sailor
CASTOR and POLYDEUCES, the Dioscuri, brothers of Helen

> (Outside the palace of the Egyptian king, THEOCLY-MENUS. In front is a monument to Proteus, his dead father. HELEN enters.)

HELEN:
These are the gleaming virgin streams
Of the Nile, which waters the Egyptian land
And fields with melted snow, not heaven's rain.
Proteus, while he lived, was king of this land,
Dwelling on the island of Pharos, though lord of Egypt. 5
He married a daughter of the sea, Psamathe,
After she left the bed of Aeacus,
And bore two children in this house,
A boy, called Theoclymenus [because he lived his life
Honoring the gods] and a noble girl, 10
Eido, her mother's pride as a baby.
When she came to marriageable age,
They called her Theonoe, for she knew
The will of the gods, now and in the future,
Receiving the gift from her ancestor, Nereus. 15

My fatherland, Sparta, is not unknown
And my father is Tyndareus. There's a story
That Zeus, taking the shape of a bird,
A swan, flew to my mother, Leda,
Making a secret marriage, having fled 20
An eagle in pursuit—if this tale is true.
I am called Helen. I will tell you
Of my terrible sufferings. Three goddesses
Came to Paris in a valley of Mount Ida,
Hera, Aphrodite, and Zeus-born Athena, 25
Wanting his judgment on their beauty.
My beauty, if misfortune is beautiful, Aphrodite
Offered in marriage to Paris, and won.
Leaving his cow shed, Paris of Ida
Came to Sparta to claim my bed. 30

Hera, angry at not overcoming the goddesses,
Voided my marriage to Paris and gave,

Helen | 79

Not me, but a breathing phantom,
Formed like me, fashioned from air,
To King Priam's son. He thinks he has me.   35
But he doesn't—only an empty image.

Zeus' plans fit well with this misery:
He brought a Greek war to the land
And to the poor Trojans, so he might lighten
Mother Earth of crowds of mortals and make   40
Known the mightiest man in Greece.

I was not there in the Trojan battle,
Just my name, a spear prize for Greeks.
Hermes took me, enfolded in air,
Hidden in a cloud—Zeus didn't forget me—   45
And placed me at this house of Proteus,
Judging him the wisest of men,
So I could keep my bed pure for Menelaus.

I am here, while my poor husband
Having marshaled an army, pursues   50
My abductor, and has gone to the towers of Troy.
Many souls have died because of me
By Scamander's streams, and I, who endure all,
Am cursed, and seem to betray my husband
And to bring on the Greeks a great war.   55

Why do I still live? I heard Hermes say
I'll dwell in the famous plain of Sparta
With my husband and he'll know I didn't
Go to Troy—but only if I don't bed another.

While Proteus saw this sunlight, I was safe   60
From marriage. Now that he is hidden
In the dark earth, the dead man's son

Wants to marry me. Honoring my husband of old,
I fall before this tomb of Proteus,
A suppliant, saving my bed for my husband.   65
If I bear a disgraceful name in Greece,
My real self shall bear no shame here.

(TEUCER enters.)

TEUCER:
Who owns this fortified palace?
It compares with the house of Plutus, the battlements
Of kings and strong-walled bastions.   70

What!
O gods, what do I see? I see the murdering
Image of that most-hated woman, who ruined
Me and all the Greeks. May the gods
Spit on you for your likeness to Helen!   75
If I were not in a foreign land, you would die
by a well-aimed arrow, for looking like Zeus' daughter.

HELEN:
Poor man, whoever you are, you turn away
And hate *me* for *her* disasters?

TEUCER:
I was wrong. I gave in to anger too much.   80
But all Greece hates Zeus' daughter.
Forgive me my words, lady.

HELEN:
Who are you? Why do you come here?

TEUCER:
One of the suffering Achaeans, my lady.

HELEN:

No wonder you hate Helen. Who are you?   85
From where? Whose son should I call you?

TEUCER:

Teucer is my name. My father Telamon
Gave me birth, and Salamis my nurturing home.

HELEN:

What brings you to the land of the Nile?

TEUCER:

I was driven out, an exile from my native land.   90

HELEN:

What torture! Who drove you out?

TEUCER:

Telamon, my father. Who could be dearer?

HELEN:

Why? That means bad luck for you.

TEUCER:

My brother, Ajax, died at Troy and destroyed me.

HELEN:

How? Not because he lost his life on your sword?   95

TEUCER:

A fall on his own sword killed him.

HELEN:

Was he mad? Who in his right mind would do this?

TEUCER:
You know of Achilles, Peleus' son?

HELEN:
Yes.
A suitor of Helen once, I hear.

TEUCER:
After his death, his friends competed for his
     weapons.   100

HELEN:
Why was this a disaster for Ajax?

TEUCER:
Another got the weapons, and he gave his life.

HELEN:
You suffer for his troubles?

TEUCER:
Because I was not destroyed with him.

HELEN:
What! Stranger, you went to famous Troy?   105

TEUCER:
Joined in sacking it, and ruined myself.

HELEN:
It is burned and destroyed by fire?

TEUCER:
Not a trace of the walls is visible.

HELEN:
O poor Helen, through you the Phrygians perished.

TEUCER:
Achaeans, too. Great atrocities were committed.   110

HELEN:
How much time has passed since the city was devastated?

TEUCER:
Almost seven fruitful cycles of the years.

HELEN:
How much longer were you in Troy?

TEUCER:
Many months. Ten years have passed.

HELEN:
Did you also take the Spartan woman?   115

TEUCER:
Menelaus took her—by the hair.

HELEN:
Did you see the wretched woman? Or hear of it?

TEUCER:
No less than I see you with my eyes.

HELEN:
Be careful you didn't have a phantom from the gods.

TEUCER:
Talk of something else. No more of her.   120

HELEN:
You think your fantasy so real?

TEUCER:
I *saw* her with my eyes! My mind sees her still.

HELEN:
Is Menelaus at home now with his wife?

TEUCER:
Neither in Argos nor by the streams of Eurotas.

HELEN:
No! You speak bad news here.   125

TEUCER:
They say he's lost with his wife.

HELEN:
Not all the Greeks made the same voyage?

TEUCER:
They did. But a storm scattered them.

HELEN:
On what stretch of open sea?

TEUCER:
While they crossed mid-ocean on the Aegean.   130

HELEN:
Did anyone see Menelaus reach shore?

TEUCER:
No one. In Greece, he is said to have died.

HELEN:
I am dead. Does Thestius' daughter live?

TEUCER:
You mean Leda? Dead and gone.

HELEN:
Surely Helen's disgrace didn't kill her?   135

TEUCER:
They say so, tying a noose about her noble neck.

HELEN:
Tyndareus' sons, do they live or not?

TEUCER:
They are dead and not dead. There are two stories.

HELEN:
Which is truer? I am wrecked by misfortune.

TEUCER:
Made into stars, they say, are gods.   140

HELEN:
Well told. What is the other story?

TEUCER:
Suicides—gave up lives because of their sister.
Enough tales. I don't want to suffer again.
Now my reason for coming to this kingly house:
I want to see the prophetess, Theonoe.   145
Be my helper. So I might get a prophecy
Where I may set favorably my full-sails

Over the sea for Cyprus, where Apollo prophesied
I shall live, giving the island the name
Salamis, after my fatherland back home.   150

HELEN:
Stranger, the voyage itself will show the way.
But flee this country before Proteus' son
Sees you, who rules this land. He is away
Following his hounds for the kill.
He also kills any Greek stranger he takes.   155
Why? Don't try to learn.
I'm silent. How would it help you?

TEUCER:
Well said, my lady. May the gods
Reward you for your goodness.
You have a body like Helen but not   160
The same heart—so very different.
May she die horribly and not reach the shore
Of the Eurotas. May *you* prosper always, lady.

        (TEUCER exits.)

HELEN:
Setting the foundations of a great lament of great sorrow,
What cry shall I compete with best? What muse shall I
        find   165
For tears or for dirges or for grief?—What misery!
O girls in feathers,
O virgins of the earth,
Sirens, if you would come
To my laments with flute   170
Or lyres or panpipes,
Tears to match my painful laments,

Helen | 87

Sorrow for sorrow, song for song!
May Persephone send
Choirs of death
In unison with my dirges,
So she might receive from me   175
Down in her dark halls
A song of thanks
In tears to my unhappy dead.

(CHORUS enters.)

CHORUS:
By dark-blue water
Upon the tangled grass,   180
Drying my purple robes,
In rays of golden sun,
On shoots of bulrushes.
There she raised a piteous cry.
I heard the noise, not fit for lyres.
Groaning, keening, she cried,   185
Like a nymph
Who calls out songs in flight
In the mountains and the rocks.
Down in the dark caves
And screams and shrieks
That she is being raped by Pan.   190

HELEN:
Misery, misery!
Spoils of a barbarian ship,
You Grecian women!
A Greek sailor
Came, came to me, bringing tears on tears.   195
The overthrow of Troy was brought

By dreadful fire, because
Of me, the murderess of many,
Because of my destructive name.
Leda took death   200
By hanging for
The agony of my shame
And my husband, wandering much on the sea,
Is dead and gone,
And Castor and his brother,   205
Twin glory of their country,
Have gone, have gone, have left
The horse-ridden plain
And field of the reedy Eurotas
Where young men wrestle.   210

CHORUS:
What misfortune!
Suffering so much your lot!
O destined woman.
Some curst fate once
Fell, fell, when Zeus flashed down on wings,   215
A snow-white swan, to father you.
What evil is not yours?
What do you not endure in life:
Your mother is no more,
Twin brothers in   220
Misfortune,
The sons of Zeus, so dear?
And you can't look upon your native land.
Reports have spread,
My queen, which hands you over   225
To a barbarian bed
And left your husband's life
To sea waves. He'll never

Make happy the halls of his father
Or bronze-housed goddess.

HELEN:
What, what Phrygian
Or man of Greece   230
Cut down the pine grieving
For Troy?
Then Priam's son fitted out
A destructive ship
And sailed with barbarian oar
To my hearth,   235
To my most-cursed
Beauty, to take me
In marriage. And murderous
Aphrodite driving death upon the Danaans—
My terrible misfortune!   240
But she on the golden throne,
Embraced and revered by Zeus,
Hera, sent the swift-footed
Son of Maia,
Who caught me up in air,
While I gathered fresh rose petals in my robe
For bronze-housed Athena,   245
Took me to this unholy land
And set wretched war—war!—between Greece
And the sons of Priam.
My fame
Beside the Simoin streams   250
Is an empty rumor.

CHORUS:
You suffer, I know. Best bear
Life's necessities as easy as you can.

HELEN:

Dear friends, what fate am I yoked with? 255
Did my mother bear me a monster to the world?
No Greek or barbarian woman bore
A white bird's egg out of herself,
As they say Leda bore me from Zeus.
And a monster has been my life and my adventures, 260
Sometimes Hera's fault, sometimes my beauty's fault.
If only I could have been washed out like a painting,
Taken an uglier form instead of beauty,
And the Greeks could have forgotten the evil fate
I live now, and not have remembered, 265
As they do, my "misfortunes."

Whoever looks to one fortune only
And is cheated by the gods—hard, but must be
        endured.
I am surrounded by many misfortunes.
First, I am innocent but maligned. 270
The nature of true evil is
To be blamed for crimes not your own.
Then the gods transported me from my fatherland
to barbarians, without friends,
And set me down a slave though born free. 275
All barbarians are slaves, except one man.

Then my fortune's anchor still held:
That my husband would come and release me.
But that is no more, since he is dead.
And my mother is destroyed, and I am the murderess, 280
Unjust as that injustice is.
And she who was the glory of my home,
My daughter, lives a virgin, manless, and gray.
The Dioscuri, said to be sons of Zeus,

Are gone. Having every misfortune,   285
I am dead. But, in fact, I am alive.
Worst of all: if I went to my homeland,
I would be barred at the gate—they thinking
I the Helen who came from Troy with Menelaus.
If my husband lives, we would recognize   290
Each other by signs known only to us.
But this won't be. He won't return safe.

Why do I live? What fate is left me?
Exchange misfortune for marriage and live
With a barbarian and sit at a luxurious table?   295
When a wife has a hateful husband,
Her body is also hateful.
Best to die. So how would I die well?
Hanging is thought disgraceful, base
Even among slaves. Cutting the throat   300
Has something noble and beautiful about it,
But hard to hit the death spot.
I have come into such a pit of evil.
Other women are fortunate in their beauty.
Mine has destroyed me.   305

CHORUS:
Helen, don't suppose that whoever
The stranger is, he told the whole truth.

HELEN:
He said clearly that my husband was dead.

CHORUS:
Many clear words prove false.

HELEN:
And the opposite: clear is true.   310

CHORUS:
You steer away from the good into misfortune.

HELEN:
Harassed by fear, I turn to fearful thoughts.

CHORUS:
How much goodwill is there for you in this house?

HELEN:
All are friends, except him who hunts me down in marriage.

CHORUS:
Here is what you do: leaving this monument . . .   315

HELEN:
What advice are you giving me?

CHORUS:
. . . Go into the house. She who knows everything,
The daughter of the sea Nereid,
Ask her about your husband: if he lives
Or has left the light. Learn your fate   320
Well, either for joy or sorrow.
Before you know anything, why
Lament? Do what I say.
Leave the tomb, meet the girl
So you shall know all. Having her   325
Here to tell the truth, why look further?
I, too, want to go into the house
And learn the virgin's prophecies.
Women must sympathize with women.

HELEN:
Friends, I'll take your advice.   330

Helen | 93

Go, go into the house
To learn there
Of my struggles.

CHORUS:
I'm willing. Don't ask twice.

HELEN:
O miserable day!   335
What crying sorrow
Will I hear?

CHORUS:
Don't anticipate, my friend,
Like a prophet, cries of sorrow.

HELEN:
What did my husband endure?   340
Does he see daylight,
The four-horsed chariot of the sun, and the courses
        of the stars,
Or under earth, among the dead,
Meet his eternal fate?   345

CHORUS:
Make the most
Of the future, whatever will happen.

HELEN:
I call upon you, I swear upon you,
Eurotas, with green water reeds,
If this death   350
Report is true
—And what is unclear?—

I shall stretch a murderous cord
Around my neck.
Or I shall drive in
The sword-killing thrust   355
Of throat-gushing slaughter,
Hard steel triumphing through my flesh,
A sacrifice to the three goddesses
And to Priam's son,
Seated in the caves of Ida once
Next to ox-stalls.

CHORUS:
May your troubles be sent elsewhere,   360
And good fortune be yours.

HELEN:
O poor Troy
Destroyed through deeds never done,
You suffered horribly. My gifts
From Aphrodite bore much blood
And many tears, brought pain on pain,   365
Tears on tears, sufferings.
Mothers lost sons. Virgins cut their hair,
Relatives of the dead,
By the swollen Phrygian Scamander.
Greece cried out, cried out,   370
Burst into keenings,
Put their hands upon their heads
And with their nails drenched
Their soft cheeks with blood.

O holy Callisto, once in Arcadia, you   375
Who came back from Zeus' bed on four moving
        paws,

How your lot was much better than my mother's.
In the form of a shaggy-limbed beast,
Softening the form with a delicate look,
You put off a painful weight.   380
Artemis drove out of the chorus
Merops' Titan daughter, as a golden-horned deer
Because of her beauty, while my looks
Wrecked, wrecked the Trojan citadel
And ruined the Greeks.   385

        (All exit.)

        (MENELAUS enters.)

MENELAUS:
O, Pelops who raced his four-horse chariot
With Oenomaus at Pisa, I wish you had given up
Your life at the feast among the gods
When you were being eaten, before
You had begotten my father Atreus,   390
Who from Aerope's bed had fathered Agamemnon
And me, Menelaus, his famous pair of sons.

I think—and this is not bragging—
I brought the greatest of armies to Troy,
Not like a king, not leading them by force at all,   395
Commanding willing young, Greek men.
We can count those no longer living
And those who escaped from the sea
And brought home the names of the dead.

On an ocean wave of gray sea,   400
I wandered miserably since I sacked
The Trojan towers. Wanting to go home,

I was thought unworthy by the gods.
I sailed to all the deserts and harbors
Of Libya. When I am near home,   405
A wind drives me back. No favorable breeze
Ever takes my sail, so I can come home.

Now miserable and shipwrecked, having
Lost companions, I was cast up here.
My ship shattered into many pieces on rocks.   410
The keel was wrenched from the strong joints,
And on it I was barely saved by chance,
Helen, too, whom I dragged from Troy.

The name of this country and its people
I don't know. I hesitated to go into the crowd   415
To ask, hiding my rags in my shame
At my misfortune. When a proud man
Fares badly, he feels more confused
Than a man long used to bad luck.

Need wears me down. No food.   420
No clothing on my body. It's obvious
What I wear are cast-off sails.
The sea took the robes I used to wear,
My shining apparel and jewels. Deep in a cave,
I hid the woman who began all   425
My trouble. I come, ordering my surviving
Friends to guard my wife.

I come alone, seeking help
For my friends there, if I can find any.
Seeing this high-walled house and the majestic   430
Gates of some rich man, I came near.
I hope to get something for my sailors

From this wealthy home. The poor
Could not help, even if they wanted to.

Hello! Some gatekeeper come out   435
And take in a troubled message.

(OLD WOMAN enters.)

OLD WOMAN:
Who's there? Won't you go off
And not stand at the court gates,
Making a row for my master. Or, being Greek,
You'll be killed. Greeks have no business here.   440

MENELAUS:
Woman. You could say it better.
I'll obey. Just give me a word.

OLD WOMAN:
Go away. This is my job, stranger,
That no one comes near the house.

MENELAUS:
Wait! Don't touch or shove me!   445

OLD WOMAN:
You don't do what I say, it's your fault.

MENELAUS:
Announce to your master that . . .

OLD WOMAN:
I'd say announcing your words would go badly.

MENELAUS:
. . . I'm a shipwrecked sailor, a sacred group.

OLD WOMAN:
Go to some other house, not this.   450

MENELAUS:
No. I'm going in. Do as I say.

OLD WOMAN:
See, you're trouble, and you'll be tossed out.

MENELAUS:
What! What's happened to my great campaigns!

OLD WOMAN:
Yes, you were famous wherever, but not here.

MENELAUS:
O lord, how I am dishonored!   455

OLD WOMAN:
Why do you wet your eyes? What makes you so
          pitiable?

MENELAUS:
My former happy fortune.

OLD WOMAN:
Why don't you give your tears to your friends?

MENELAUS:
What country is this? Whose barbarian home?

OLD WOMAN:
This is Proteus' house. The land of Egypt.   460

MENELAUS:
Egypt! Poor me, where have I sailed?

OLD WOMAN:
What's wrong with the glorious Nile?

MENELAUS:
I don't blame that. I lament my fate.

OLD WOMAN:
Many fare badly, not you alone.

MENELAUS:
Is your ruler at home?   465

OLD WOMAN:
This is his monument. His son rules the land.

MENELAUS:
Where is he? Out, or in the house?

OLD WOMAN:
Not here. He's most hostile to Greeks.

MENELAUS:
What did I do to deserve that?

OLD WOMAN:
Helen is in the house, Zeus' daughter.   470

MENELAUS:
What? What are you saying? Tell me again.

OLD WOMAN:
Tyndareus' daughter, who was at Sparta.

MENELAUS:
Where did she come from? What do you mean?

OLD WOMAN:
She came here from Lacedaemon.

MENELAUS:
When? I have been robbed of my wife from the cave?   475

OLD WOMAN:
O stranger, it was before the Achaeans went to Troy.
But get from the house. Things have changed here.
The royal house is troubled.
You come at a bad time. If the king captures you,
Hospitality for you will be death.   480
I like Greeks, even if I speak
Harshly. I fear my master.

          (OLD WOMAN exits.)

MENELAUS:
What am I to think? What to say? I hear
Bad news on top of old,
If, since fighting at Troy, I come   485
Taking my wife who is kept in a cave,
And some other woman having
The same name lives in this house.
She said she was Zeus' child.
Some other man has Zeus' name   490
By the Nile? But there's only the one in heaven.
Where on earth is Sparta but where
Eurotas' streams and beautiful reeds are?

Tyndareus is the name of *one* man.
Another land has the same name Lacedaemon,   495
Another Troy, too? I don't know what to say.
In the wide world, many men have
The same names it seems. So do cities,
And women. It's not amazing at all.

I'm not running from the terrors of a servant.
No man is so barbarous in his heart that, hearing   500
My name, won't give me a piece of meat.
The torching of Troy is famous, and I, Menelaus,
Torched it. I'm not nobody *anywhere*.
I shall wait for the lord of the house. I need   505
To watch for two things. If he's a savage,
I'll disappear back to the shipwreck.
If he shows any compassion, I'll ask for
Provisions for my present misfortune.
For me, a king, this is my worst   510
Moment: to ask another king
For help. But I must. Those are not
My words, but wisdom itself.
Nothing is stronger than terrible necessity.

(CHORUS enters from the palace.)

CHORUS:
I heard from the mantic girl.   515
What I wanted
Entering the king's house: that Menelaus
Has not, covered with earth,
Yet gone through black-lit Erebus,
But worn down   520
By salty waves,

Has not yet reached home port,
Enduring all,
A wayward life and friendless,
Setting foot in every land,   525
His oar in the sea
Ever since Troy.

(HELEN enters from the palace.)

HELEN:
Now I come back to the seat
At the tomb, after learning the joyous words
Of Theonoe, who truly knows all.   530
She says my husband lives in the daylight.
He wanders by sail, in endless journeys
Everywhere, exhausted by traveling,
And he shall come when he reaches the end of his
        suffering.
One thing she didn't say: if he will live   535
After he arrives. I didn't ask this directly,
Glad that she said he was safe for now.
She said he was near this land,
Cast up a shipwreck with few friends.
O when will you come? How welcome you will be!   540

Wait! Who is this? Am I not being trapped
By the unholy, plotting son of Proteus?
Shall I not set my foot in the god's tomb,
Fast as a young mare or the god's bacchante.
He has a wild look, my stalker.   545

MENELAUS:
You there, desperately trying to reach

The base of the tomb and the pillars of sacrifice,
Stop! Why are you running? Seeing
You appear, I'm confused, and speechless.

HELEN:
I'm ruined, my women. I'm kept away   550
From the tomb by this man. He wishes
To give me in marriage to the king I'm avoiding.

MENELAUS:
I'm no thief or servant of bad men.

HELEN:
But you are wearing rags.

MENELAUS:
Don't be afraid. Stop running.   555

HELEN:
I have, since I have touched the tomb.

MENELAUS:
Who are you? Whose face do I see, woman?

HELEN:
And you? We have the same question.

MENELAUS:
Never was a figure more like hers!

HELEN:
Oh gods! To know your friends is a divine gift!   560

MENELAUS:
Are you a Hellene, or some native woman?

HELEN:
A Hellene, but I want to know what you are.

MENELAUS:
I see you look so like Helen, my lady.

HELEN:
And you like Menelaus. I don't know what to say.

MENELAUS:
You recognize the most unfortunate of men.   565

HELEN:
Finally, you come into your wife's arms.

MENELAUS:
What wife? Don't touch my clothes.

HELEN:
The one Tyndareus, my father, gave you.

MENELAUS:
O blazing Hecate, send a favorable vision!

HELEN:
I'm no night servant of the Wayward Goddess.   570

MENELAUS:
I'm not a husband with two wives.

HELEN:
What *other* wife are you lord of?

MENELAUS:
The one in the cave. I took her from Troy.

HELEN:
No other woman is your wife but me.

MENELAUS:
Am I in my right mind? Are my eyes bad?   575

HELEN:
Seeing me, you don't think you see your wife?

MENELAUS:
The same form, but I am not certain.

HELEN:
Look close. What more do you need?

MENELAUS:
You are like her. I won't deny it.

HELEN:
What but your eyes will teach you?   580

MENELAUS:
My trouble is I have another wife.

HELEN:
I didn't go to Troy. That was a phantom.

MENELAUS:
And *who* makes living bodies?

HELEN:
It was air, the god-made wife you had.

MENELAUS:
What god made it? You speak nonsense.   585

HELEN:
Hera made a substitute, so Paris wouldn't take me.

MENELAUS:
What? You were here and in Troy at the same time?

HELEN:
The name could be in many places, not the body.

MENELAUS:
Let me go. I've had enough trouble.

HELEN:
You leave me for a bed of air?   590

MENELAUS:
I hope you fare well, since you look like Helen.

HELEN:
I'm ruined. I find you and have no husband.

MENELAUS:
My great suffering at Troy convinces me. Not you.

HELEN:
Ah me! Who is worse off?
My dearest friends leave me, and I won't   595
Go to Greece or my fatherland ever.

(SERVANT enters.)

SERVANT:
Menelaus, searching everywhere, wandering
The whole barbarian land, I almost missed you.
I was sent by the companions you left behind.

MENELAUS:
What is it? You weren't attacked by barbarians?   600

SERVANT:
A miracle, though that word is too weak.

MENELAUS:
Speak, since you bring news in such haste.

SERVANT:
You endured great pain for nothing.

MENELAUS:
You sing old misery. What's your message?

SERVANT:
Your wife has vanished, caught up   605
Into the depths of the air, hidden in the sky.
Leaving the sacred cave where we kept her,
She said, "O miserable Phrygians
And all you Achaeans, you died for me,

A trick of Hera's, on Scamander's shores,   610
Thinking Paris had Helen. He didn't.
I, having waited my allotted time,
As was necessary, go up to my father,
The sky. Poor Tyndareus' daughter has heard
Of her bad reputation, though she is pure and blameless."   615

Oh! Good day, daughter of Leda. You were here?
I announced that you went high in the stars,
Not knowing you had wings on.
I must not let you mock us again.
You brought pain enough   620
To your husband and his allies at Troy.

MENELAUS:
That's it! Her words hit upon
The truth. O long-awaited day
Which gave her into my arms!

HELEN:
O dearest of men, Menelaus, how long   625
It was, and what joy now!
I take my newfound husband, friends,
Embrace him in my loving arms
After the long, burning days.

MENELAUS:
And I you! Having so much to tell,   630
I don't know where to begin now.

HELEN:
I'm elated. My hair
Tingles and tears fall.

I throw my arms about you. What happiness!
O, husband, I hold you!   635

MENELAUS:
O beloved sight, I find no fault in you.
I hold my wife, born of Zeus and Leda.

HELEN:
My brothers on white horses in torchlight
Thought us happy, happy.   640

MENELAUS:
Then a god took you away from my home,
Leads you to
A greater fortune.

HELEN:
An evil good brought us together, my husband,
A long time, but still may I enjoy my fortune.   645

MENELAUS:
May you indeed. I pray with you.
One of two can't be miserable, the other not.

HELEN:
My friends, my friends,
No more do I lament or suffer for the past.
I have the husband that I waited for   650
Many years to come from Troy.

MENELAUS:
You hold me, and I hold you. Barely surviving
The many days, I recognize the work of the goddess.

HELEN:
My tears are joyous. More full
Of gratitude than pain.   655

MENELAUS:
What can I say? What mortal could hope for this?

HELEN:
Beyond belief, I hold you to my breast.

MENELAUS:
And I you, who seemed to go to the Idaean
City and the miserable towers of Troy.
By the gods, how were you taken from my home?   660

HELEN:
What a bitter trail you start on!
What a bitter story you ask for!

MENELAUS:
Speak. It should be heard. All things are gifts of the gods.

HELEN:
I spit upon such a tale,
Such a tale as I bring forth!

MENELAUS:
Speak nevertheless. It is sweet to hear past troubles.   665

HELEN:
No oar flew me to a young
Barbarian bed. No desire flew me
To an illegal marriage.

MENELAUS:
What god or destiny tore you from your city?

HELEN:
O husband, Zeus', Zeus' son and Maia's son,   670
Hermes brought me to the Nile.

MENELAUS:
Incredible! Who sent him? What terrifying words!

HELEN:
I'm soaking my eyes with tears.
The wife of Zeus ruined me.

MENELAUS:
Hera? Why did she want to hurt us?   675

HELEN:
I was cursed by the fountain of those cleansing waters,
Where the goddesses made their bodies glisten
When they came for judgment.

MENELAUS:
Hera made the judgment trouble for you?

HELEN:
To take me from Paris.   680

MENELAUS:
                    What? Tell me!

HELEN:
Aphrodite promised me to him.

MENELAUS:

                         What misery.

HELEN:
So miserable, miserable me she sent to Egypt.

MENELAUS:
She put a phantom in your place, as you said.

HELEN:
And the suffering, suffering of your house,
Mother, poor me!

MENELAUS:

                    What are you saying?   685

HELEN:
Mother's no more. She strangled herself in a noose
Because of the shame of my disgraceful marriage.

MENELAUS:
Good god! What of our daughter, Hermione?

HELEN:
Marriageless, childless, my lord,
She bewails my shame, a marriageless marriage.   690

MENELAUS:
O Paris, you destroyed my house completely!

HELEN:
That, and you, and countless
Bronze-weaponed Danaans.

The god tore me from country, from city,
From you, to cursed misfortune,   695
When I left home and bed—which I didn't leave—
For a shameful marriage.

CHORUS:
If you hit good fortune in the future,
It shall make up for the past.

SERVANT:
Menelaus, let me share in the joy.   700
I understand, but not clearly.

MENELAUS:
Yes, old man. Share in our story.

SERVANT:
Is she not the cause of trouble in Troy?

MENELAUS:
Not her. I was tricked by the gods. I held
In my arms an evil image of cloud.   705

SERVANT:
What are you saying?
We suffered only for a cloud?

MENELAUS:
Hera's work and a contest of three goddesses.

SERVANT:
What? Is this truly your wife?

MENELAUS:
It's her. Believe my words.   710

SERVANT:
O daughter, the god, who is like some
Many-colored enigma, guides all somehow,
Turning this way and that. One man suffers.
Another does not, but comes to ruin in the end.
Nothing is steady in his ever-evolving fate.   715
You and your husband had suffering:
You through reputation; he through battle lust.
Driving on then, he got nothing. Now faring
His best, he gets joy by chance.

You do not shame your old father, or your brothers,   720
Not having done what is famous now.
I remember your marriage song again.
I recall the torches I carried running
With the horses and you, a bride,   725
With him in the chariot, leaving your wealthy home.
He is evil who does not honor his master,
Joy in his joy and share his troubles.
I, even though born a slave, would be counted
A noble servant. Though not free in name,   730
I'm free in mind. Better this, than one person suffer
Two evils at once: to have an evil heart
And to hear from one's neighbors that one is a slave.

MENELAUS:
Come, old man, at my shield,
You toiled hard for me.   735
Now enjoy my success.

Go announce to my remaining friends
What you discovered here, our good fortune,
And to remain on the shore and await
My coming trials, as I expect,   740
If I can steal this woman from the land,
And find how we, united in fortune,
Can be safe from the barbarians.

SERVANT:
So be it, my lord. But I know
How ridiculous and full of lies prophecies are.   745
Nothing is sound in the holy fires.
Bird cries are unclear. To believe
Birds help men is simpleminded.
Calchas said or hinted none of this
To the army, seeing his friends die for a cloud,   750
Or Helenus, though his country was annihilated for
     nothing.
You could say, "The god doesn't want it known."
Why then do we consult prophets? We need to sacrifice
And ask the gods for gifts and forget divination.
That's an old fraud for moneymaking.   755
No one becomes rich on divination without effort.
The best prophet is intelligence and common sense.

     (SERVANT exits.)

CHORUS:
I am of the same mind as the old man
On prophecies. Having the gods for friends
Makes the best prophecy for the home.   760

HELEN:
Yes! Things have gone well here.
To know how you were saved from Troy,

Poor man, has no value here. But loved ones
Wish to hear of their beloved's suffering.

MENELAUS:
In that one word and one journey, you ask much.   765
Why should I tell of wreckage on the Aegean,
The deadly watch fires of Nauplius in Euboea,
The cities in Crete and Libya I visited,
The lookout of Perseus? I would overwhelm
You with words. Telling you, I would grieve   770
As I suffered then. I would be devastated twice.

HELEN:
You spoke better than I asked.
Tell me one thing. Let the rest go.
How long did you wander wrecked on the wide sea?

MENELAUS:
I was in the ships at Troy ten years,   775
And I wandered seven more.

HELEN:
How horrible! You speak of a long time, poor man.
Saved there, you come to slaughter here.

MENELAUS:
What! What do you mean? You've destroyed me, my
            lady.

HELEN:
As quickly as you can, flee from this land.   780
You will be killed by the man of this house.

MENELAUS:
What did I do to win this misfortune?

HELEN:
Unexpectedly, you got in the way of my marriage.

MENELAUS:
What! Someone wishes to marry my wife?

HELEN:
Wishes to violate me, a violation I must endure.   785

MENELAUS:
Someone acting on his own or the country's ruler?

HELEN:
Proteus' son, the ruler of the land.

MENELAUS:
I understand the gatekeeper's riddle!

HELEN:
At what barbarian gate were you standing?

MENELAUS:
This one. Where I was driven off like a beggar.   790

HELEN:
You were begging bread? Poor me!

MENELAUS:
That's what it was, though not by name.

HELEN:
You know everything, it seems, about my marriage.

MENELAUS:
I know. Whether you escaped his bed, I'm not sure.

HELEN:
Know I am saved, untouched, for you.   795

MENELAUS:
What proof is there? Nice to hear, if true.

HELEN:
You see my wretched seat at this tomb?

MENELAUS:
I see a miserable straw bed. What's this to you?

HELEN:
I come here as a suppliant, fleeing *his* bed.

MENELAUS:
Lacking an altar, or for a barbarian custom?   800

HELEN:
This protected me, like a temple of the gods.

MENELAUS:
Can't I take you home by sea?

HELEN:
A sword waits for you, not my bed.

MENELAUS:
I am the most wretched of men!

HELEN:
Forget shame, and run from this land.   805

MENELAUS:
Leaving you? After sacking Troy for your sake.

HELEN:
Better than dying for my marriage.

MENELAUS:
What you say is unmanly and unworthy of Troy.

HELEN:
You wouldn't kill the king. Probably you want to.

MENELAUS:
Can his body not be broken by iron?   810

HELEN:
You'll see. To dare the impossible is not wise.

MENELAUS:
Shall I have my hands bound quietly?

HELEN:
You are at an impasse. You need a plan.

MENELAUS:
It's sweeter to die acting than not acting.

HELEN:
We have only one hope of being saved.   815

MENELAUS:
By money, or daring, or words?

HELEN:
If the king doesn't know you arrived.

MENELAUS:
I know he won't know me. Who will tell him?

HELEN:
He has an ally inside equal to the gods.

MENELAUS:
An oracle set in the inner sanctum?   820

HELEN:
No. His sister. They call her Theonoe.

MENELAUS:
Her name is oracular. Tell me what she does.

HELEN:
She knows all and will tell her brother you are here.

MENELAUS:
I am a dead man. It's impossible to escape her notice.

HELEN:
Perhaps we could convince her as suppliants . . .   825

MENELAUS:
To do what? What hope are you giving me?

HELEN:
. . . Not to tell her brother you are in the country.

MENELAUS:
Once she's persuaded, we can leave the land?

HELEN:
With her aid, easily. Without her knowledge, no.

MENELAUS:
That's your undertaking. Woman to woman.   830

HELEN:
Her knees will not be untouched by my hands.

MENELAUS:
What if she rejects our plea?

HELEN:
You die, and wretched me marries by force.

MENELAUS:
You betray me! Force is your excuse.

HELEN:
I swear a holy oath upon your head.   835

MENELAUS:
What! To die? Never change husbands?

HELEN:
With the same sword, I shall lie beside you.

MENELAUS:
For this, touch my right hand.

HELEN:
I touch it. Your death eclipses my light.

MENELAUS:
If you are gone, I end my life.   840

HELEN:
How can we die and gain glory?

MENELAUS:
I'll kill you on this tomb. Then kill myself.

First, I shall wage a fierce battle
Over your marriage. Let any challenger come near.
I shall not disgrace my Trojan reputation,   845
Nor going to Greece, bear great blame,
I, who deprived Thetis of Achilles,
Saw Telemonian Ajax slaughtered,
And Nestor childless. For my wife
Shall I not think it worthy to die?   850
Yes, indeed. If the gods be wise,
They bury a strong-souled man who perished
In battle with a light cover of earth,
And throw a coward on a hard rock.

CHORUS:
May this race of Tantalus have good fortune.   855
May trouble change its course.

HELEN:
Miserable me! What fortune is mine.
Menelaus, we are at the end. The prophetess,
Theonoe, comes out of the house,
And the house resounds to the door bars' release.   860
Run! But why must we escape?
Whether she's present or elsewhere, she knows
You are here. Unfortunate you! I'm ruined.
Saved from barbarian Troy, you fall in
Again with barbarian swords.

(THEONOE enters with SERVANTS.)

THEONOE:
Lead on, bringing the blazing torches.   865
Burn pure with sulfur the farthest sky
In holy rites, so we may receive heaven's pure air.
You there, if anyone has defiled the path

Helen | 123

With impure foot, touch it with cleansing flame,
Strike with the pine torch, so I may pass through.   870
Having performed your duty to the gods,
Bring the hearth fire back inside.

(SERVANTS perform rites and exit.)

Helen, my prophecies? How are they?
Your husband, Menelaus, is really here,
His ships lost and your phantom vanished.   875

Poor man, what trouble you flee and come to.
You don't know if you will return home or stay here.
There is strife among the gods and an assembly
Concerning you, at Zeus' seat, this very day.
Hera, hostile to you before, is kind now   880
And wishes to save you for home
With this woman, so Greece may learn Aphrodite's
Gift of marriage to Paris was fraudulent.
But Aphrodite wishes to ruin your return,
So she's not put to the test nor revealed to have bought   885
Her beauty prize with Helen by a useless marriage.
The end is up to me: either what Aphrodite wants,
That I tell my brother you are here and destroy you,
Or I stand with Hera and save your life,
Hiding you from my brother who appointed me   890
To tell him when you journeyed to this land.
Who will send a message to my brother
That this man is here, so I am not in danger?

HELEN:
O virgin, I fall suppliant at your knees.
I kneel in this unfortunate way for myself   895
And this man, whom at long last I found.

I am about to see him die.
Please don't report my husband to your brother,
My beloved just come into my arms.
Save him, I pray you. Do not betray   900
For your brother, your former holiness,
Buying evil and unjust gratitude.
Gods hate violence, and they order
Everyone not to possess stolen property.
Any unjust wealth is to go untouched.   905
The sky is common to all men, and the earth,
Where they fill their houses with possessions,
And should not take from others, or lose by force.

Timely for us, wretched for me,
Hermes gave me to your father to save   910
For my husband, who is here and wants me back
Dead, how can he take me? How could
Your father give the living to the dead?
Think what the gods and your father would do:
Whether a god or the dead man would want,   915
Or not want, to give back what belongs to another.
I think yes. So you should not respect
A rash brother more than a worthy father.
If you are a prophet and know the gods
And overthrow your father's justice   920
And grace your unjust brother, it is shameful
For you to know all the gods so well
And the future and not what is just.

Rescue me from torment, the pain
I lie in, add to my good fortune.   925
There is no mortal who does not hate Helen.
In Greece, they say I betrayed my husband
And went to live in Phrygian luxury.

If I went to Greece, set foot in Sparta,
Hearing, seeing themselves wrecked by the plans 930
Of the gods and that I was not the betrayer of loved
     ones,
They would give me back again my virtue.
And I would give my daughter in marriage,
Whom no one wants. Leaving this bitter journey
Here, I shall enjoy the happiness of home. 935

If this man were dead on the pyre,
Far away, I would love him with tears.
Shall I lose him, alive now and saved?
No, virgin, I beg of you!
Do me this favor and imitate the ways 940
Of your just father. This is the greatest fame
For children: whoever is born
Of a kind father, turns out the same.

CHORUS:
These words are to be pitied,
And you, also. I want to hear 945
Menelaus' words for his own life.

MENELAUS:
I dare not fall at your knee
Or wet my eyes with tears. I would be
Cowardly and shame Troy most of all.
They say it is right for a noble man 950
To let tears fall from his eyes in misfortune.
I shall not choose that honor,
If it is honor, but the way of a great soul.
If it seems best to you to save me, a stranger
Rightly trying to take back my wife, 955
Give me her, and save my life, too. If not,

Not for the first time, but as often, I am locked
In struggle, and you are shown an evil woman.

I believe what is noble and just in me
Will touch your heart most, as I fall   960
At your father's monument, saying,
Old man, who inhabits this stone tomb,
Give her back. I ask you for my wife
Whom Zeus sent here for you to save.
I know, being dead, you no longer give her up.   965
This woman will not think it right
That her once esteemed father, called up
From below, be defamed. Now she has the power.

O Hades in hell, I call you for ally.
You who, for my wife, received many men   970
Fallen in my slaughtering. You have your payment for
    her.
Either give back these men alive
Or force this woman to show herself greater
Than her father in giving back my wife.

If you plan to steal her   975
I shall say what she left out:
We are locked in oaths—so you may know,
O virgin—first to battle your brother.
He or I must die. That is all.
If he does not oppose my strength, step by step,   980
And, as we supplicate, he hunts us with starvation,
I have resolved to kill this woman, then to thrust
This double blade into my gut
On top of this tomb, so streams of blood
Will drip down the monument. The two of us   985
Will lie corpses, side to side, on the cut-stone tomb,

Helen

Eternal pain for you and a censure on your father.
No one marries this woman, not your brother,
No one. But I shall lead her away,
If not home, then to the house of the dead.   990

Why say this? Turning womanish with tears,
I would be more pitiable than heroic.

Kill, if you think best. You don't kill an infamous
        man.
But, better, be persuaded by my words
So you may be just and I take my wife.   995

CHORUS:
It is yours to judge his words, young lady.
Judge so as to please all.

THEONOE:
I was born to do right, and I wish to.
I shall honor myself and not disgrace
My father's fame, nor honor my brother   1000
In a way that will appear dishonorable.
A great temple of justice lies in
My heart. I received it from Nereus,
And I shall try to preserve it, Menelaus.
I will cast my vote with Hera   1005
Who wishes to do you well. May Aphrodite
Be kind to me, though we have nothing in common.
I shall try to remain a virgin always.
Those reproaches on the tomb of my father
Are my words, too. I would be unjust,   1010
If I did not give her back. Alive, he would
Give her back to you and you to her.
There is retribution among those below

As among those above. The mind
Of the dead doesn't live, but it holds   1015
Immortal thought permeating immortal air.

To be brief, I shall be silent
About your supplication, nor shall I be
An accomplice to the lust of my brother.
I will do him a kindness, while not seeming to,   1020
If I turn him from impiety to righteousness.

You yourselves discover a way,
And I shall stand aside silently.
Begin with the goddesses. Supplicate
Aphrodite to let you return home   1025
And the mind of Hera to remain the same:
Safety for you and your husband.

And you, O dead father, as long as I have power,
Never may you be called impious rather than righteous.

(THEONOE exits.)

CHORUS:
No one ever prospered, being unjust,   1030
And in justice lies the hope of safety.

HELEN:
Menelaus, we are saved by the virgin.
We must bring our ideas together
Into one common plan of escape.

MENELAUS:
Listen. You have been long familiar   1035
With the servants in the king's household.

HELEN:
What do you mean? You hope
To do something helpful to us both.

MENELAUS:
Might you persuade someone in charge
Of the four-horse chariots to give us one?   1040

HELEN:
I could. But what route could we take,
Not knowing the barbarian plains?

MENELAUS:
Yes. That's impossible. What if I hid in the house
And killed the king with this two-edged sword?

HELEN:
His sister won't let you nor keep silent   1045
About your going to murder her brother.

MENELAUS:
There is not even a ship in which
We might escape. The sea owns ours.

HELEN:
Listen—if a woman can say anything wise.
Not dead in reality, do you want to be dead in name?   1050

MENELAUS:
A bird of ill omen. But if it helps me, speak.
Alive, I'm ready to die in words.

HELEN:
I shall mourn you with a woman's shorn hair
And with lamentations in front of the unholy man.

MENELAUS:
How does this help our escape? 1055
Your scheme is a bit old-fashioned.

HELEN:
I will ask the king of this land to bury
You in an empty tomb because you died at sea.

MENELAUS:
And he grants it. Then how will we escape
Without a ship and my tomb being empty? 1060

HELEN:
I'll order him to give us a ship
To send the offerings into the sea's embrace.

MENELAUS:
Well said, except: If he orders
To set the tomb on land, the plan fails.

HELEN:
I shall say in Greece it's forbidden 1065
To bury on land those who died at sea.

MENELAUS:
Right again. Then I shall sail, too,
And will put the offerings in the same ship.

HELEN:
You must certainly be there and
Your sailors who survived shipwreck. 1070

MENELAUS:
If I have a ship at anchor, man
By man will stand, bearing a sword.

HELEN:
You must arrange everything. If only there may be
Favorable winds for our sails and a fast ship.

MENELAUS:
Let it be so. The gods are stopping my suffering. 1075
But from whom will you learn that I am dead?

HELEN:
From you. Say you alone sailing with the son
Of Atreus escaped fate and saw him die.

MENELAUS:
Yes, and these rags around my body
Will witness your shipwreck story. 1080

HELEN:
They're timely now, though destructive before.
Maybe that suffering will prove favorable.

MENELAUS:
Should I go into the house with you,
Or calmly sit by this monument?

HELEN:
Stay here. If he does anything outrageous to you, 1085
This tomb, and your sword, will save you.
Going back into the house, I'll cut my hair,
Change my white robe to black,
And drive my bloody nails into my cheeks.
It's a grand contest. I see two falls of the scales: 1090
Either I must die, caught scheming,
Or I go home, saving your life.

O Queen Hera, who lies in Zeus' bed,
Revive from pain two pitiful creatures.
We ask you, throwing our arms straight   1095
To the sky, where you live in spangled stars.
And you, who won beauty by my marriage,
Aphrodite, daughter of Dione, don't murder me.
You have outraged me enough before,
Offering my name, not myself, to the barbarians.   1100
Let me die, if you wish to kill me,
In my native land. Why are you ever greedy for crime,
Lust, trickery, deceit, and plots,
Decorating homes with charms of blood?
Were you only moderate! In every other way,   1105
You're the sweetest goddess for mankind. I won't deny it.

(HELEN exits.)

CHORUS:
I cry to you, who sit
In your tree home,
The muses' temple, your seat,
The tuneful,
Most-gifted bird,
Tearful nightingale.   1110
O, come trilling through your tan throat,
My helper in lament,
As I sing Helen's
Dreadful pain, the weeping fate
Of Trojan women   1115
Beneath the Greek spears,
Paris driving gray waves with barbarian oar,
When he came and brought your marriage bed from Sparta
And misery for Priam's sons,

O, Helen: Paris' fatal marriage,   1120
By the connivance of Aphrodite.

So many Greeks were killed
By the flung stones
And spears to live in dark Hades,
Their wretched
Wives with shorn hair.
Homes lie husbandless.   1125
Alone, Nauplius fired sea-washed Euboea
With flame on flame and killed
Many Greeks and smashed
Them on rocks in Caphereus
Upon the headlands   1130
With a false star.
Menelaus, thrown far to grim, harborless
Lands by blasts, far storms, where barbarian dress is
        worn,
He carried a prize, no prize, but strife
Inside the ships of the Danaans,   1135
The holy phantom that Hera made.

What is god, or not god, or half-god,
What mortal searcher can say?
He discovers the utmost limit who knows the works
        of gods   1140
Jump here, again there, in contradictory
And unexpected fortunes.
You, O Helen, were born the daughter of Zeus.
Your winged father begot you   1145
In Leda's womb
And then you were proclaimed in Greece:
Betrayer, unfaithful, unjust, ungodly.

Nor is there a certain and true word that I have ever
      discovered
About the gods from mortals.   1150

You are mad who win fame in war work
With mighty points on your spears
And who foolishly put an end to the pains of war with
      death.
War will not leave city-states, if blood is judge   1155
Of every contest—never!
War would have spared in Troy the bedrooms of Priam,
If talk could possibly have settled
Your war, O Helen.   1160
Now some are in the care of Hades
Below, and a murdering flame, like Zeus,'
Rushes over walls. You endure suffering on top of hard
      suffering
In pitiful disasters.

      (THEOCLYMENUS enters with SERVANTS.)

THEOCLYMENUS:
Greetings to my father's tomb. I buried you,   1165
Proteus, by the doors, so I might address you.
Going and coming from the house, I,
Your son, Theoclymenus, always greet you.
 —Take care of the dogs and hunting nets,
My men, in the royal palace.—   1170

      (SERVANTS exit.)

Many times I have cursed myself
For not punishing these bastards with death.

Now I learn some Greek has come
Openly into the land and my guards didn't notice,
A spy or someone hunting for Helen.   1175
He dies—if only he be caught.

What!

It seems I find the business finished.
Leaving her seat by the tomb empty,
Tyndareus' daughter has been taken over the sea.
Attention! Release the bars! Open   1180
The stables, servants, and bring out the chariots!
So she won't slip from the country without
Our efforts, she I desire for wife.

(HELEN enters.)

Wait! I see her we pursue,
Here in the house and not escaping.   1185
You! Why have you put on black,
Changing from white, and from your noble head
Cut hair, laying on the knife,
Wetting your cheeks with bright tears.
Were you convinced by a dream   1190
In the night and cry out, or did you hear
Some bad news from home that broke your heart?

HELEN:
My lord—I name you that now—I am ruined.
My world is gone. I am nothing anymore.

THEOCLYMENUS:
What trouble are you in? What misfortune?   1195

HELEN:
My Menelaus—how can I say it?—is dead.

THEOCLYMENUS:
I don't rejoice in your words, though they're my good
     fortune.
How do you know? Did Theonoe say this?

HELEN:
That man said it who was there when he died.

THEOCLYMENUS:
Someone came who announced this for certain?   1200

HELEN:
He came. Would he would go where I want him to go!

THEOCLYMENUS:
Who is he? Where is he? So I may learn for sure.

HELEN:
That's him crouching at the tomb.

THEOCLYMENUS:
Apollo! How ugly his clothes are!

HELEN:
I suppose my husband dressed like that.   1205

THEOCLYMENUS:
What is his country? From where did he put in to
     shore?

HELEN:
A Greek, one of the Achaeans sailing with my husband.

THEOCLYMENUS:
What kind of death did he say Menelaus had?

Helen

HELEN:
The worst. In the watery surf of the sea.

THEOCLYMENUS:
Where on the barbarous seas was he carried?   1210

HELEN:
Libya. Driven out on the shelterless rocks.

THEOCLYMENUS:
How was he not destroyed, sharing the same voyage?

HELEN:
Sometimes commoners are luckier than aristocrats.

THEOCLYMENUS:
Where is the wrecked ship he left?

HELEN:
Where may it perish completely! But not Menelaus.   1215

THEOCLYMENUS:
That man is dead. In what boat did the other come?

HELEN:
Sailors found him and took him up, he says.

THEOCLYMENUS:
Where is that cursed one sent to Troy instead of
          you?

HELEN:
You mean the cloud image? Vanished in air.

THEOCLYMENUS:
O Priam and the land of Troy, fallen for nothing!   1220

HELEN:
And I suffered misfortune with Priam's sons.

THEOCLYMENUS:
Did he leave your husband unburied or cover him with
          earth?

HELEN:
Unburied. O my dreadful suffering!

THEOCLYMENUS:
For this you cut your golden hair?

HELEN:
He is dear to me, once being here alive.   1225

THEOCLYMENUS:
It's proper to weep this misfortune.

HELEN:
You think it's easy to trick your sister?

THEOCLYMENUS:
No, it's not. So. Will you remain at the tomb?

HELEN:
Escaping you, I'm faithful to my husband.   1230

THEOCLYMENUS:
You mock me and don't leave the dead?

HELEN:
But no longer. Prepare my marriage.

THEOCLYMENUS:
A long time coming. But nevertheless I commend you.

HELEN:
Here is what you do: let us forget the past.

THEOCLYMENUS:
How? Let favor follow favor.

HELEN:
Let us make a truce and reconcile ourselves.   1235

THEOCLYMENUS:
I put aside my fight with you, Let it fly away.

HELEN:
Now on my knees, since you are dear to me . . .

THEOCLYMENUS:
Why do you hunt me down and supplicate me?

HELEN:
. . . I wish to bury my dead husband.

THEOCLYMENUS:
What! A tomb for the lost or to bury a ghost?   1240

HELEN:
It's the custom for Greeks who die at sea.

THEOCLYMENUS:
What do you do? Pelops' sons are wise in this.

HELEN:
Bury him in an empty woolen robe.

THEOCLYMENUS:
Honor him. Set it anywhere in the land.

HELEN:
We don't bury dead sailors that way.   1245

THEOCLYMENUS:
How? I don't know Greek customs.

HELEN:
We bring out to sea whatever the dead need.

THEOCLYMENUS:
What then can I provide for the dead man?

HELEN:
This man knows. I'm at a loss, being fortunate till now.

THEOCLYMENUS:
Stranger, you brought a good report.   1250

MENELAUS:
Not good for me, or the dead man.

THEOCLYMENUS:
How do you bury the dead who die at sea?

MENELAUS:
According to the man's wealth at the time.

THEOCLYMENUS:
Name the price you want for her sake.

MENELAUS:
First, sacrifice blood to those below.   1255

THEOCLYMENUS:
Sacrifice what? Tell me and I shall do it.

MENELAUS:
You decide. Whatever you give will do.

THEOCLYMENUS:
A horse or bull is the barbarian custom.

MENELAUS:
Give, but give nothing deformed.

THEOCLYMENUS:
We have no shortage of rich herds.   1260

MENELAUS:
You must supply a made bed without a body.

THEOCLYMENUS:
Be it so. What else does custom demand?

MENELAUS:
Bronze weapons, for he was a friend of the spear.

Helen

THEOCLYMENUS:
What we give will be worthy of Pelops' sons.

MENELAUS:
And whatever is beautiful that earth bears.   1265

THEOCLYMENUS:
Then what? How do you throw it into the waves?

MENELAUS:
We need a ship and skilled rowers.

THEOCLYMENUS:
How far from land will the ship be?

MENELAUS:
So the oar splash is hardly seen from shore.

THEOCLYMENUS:
Why? Why does Greece honor this custom?   1270

MENELAUS:
So waves don't send back pollution to land.

THEOCLYMENUS:
There'll be a fast Phoenician ship.

MENELAUS:
That would be fine, and good for Menelaus.

THEOCLYMENUS:
Can't you do this without her?

MENELAUS:
It's a task for mother or wife or children.   1275

THEOCLYMENUS:
It's her job, as you say, to bury her husband.

MENELAUS:
For piety's sake, don't rob the dead of their rites.

THEOCLYMENUS:
Let her go. I want to nurture a pious wife.
Go in, someone, and bring out the corpse offerings.
And you, I won't send away empty-handed   1280
For what you've done for her. For bringing me
Good news, you'll receive clothes,
To replace your rags, and food, so you can go home,
Because I see how bad off you are.

You, poor woman, don't waste yourself
On the useless. Menelaus met his fate.   1285
The dead can't live through weeping.

MENELAUS:
It's up to you, young woman. You must oblige
Your present husband and let the lost one go.
That's what is best for you in this case.   1290
If I reach Greece safely, I'll remove
Your former stigma—if you become
The wife you should to your husband.

HELEN:
So be it. My husband will never blame me.
You, being there, will learn that.   1295
But, poor man, go in and bathe,

And change your clothing. Without delay,
I'll treat you well. You shall perform the offerings
For my beloved Menelaus better
If you get from me what you deserve.   1300

(HELEN, MENELAUS, and THEOCLYMENUS exit.)

CHORUS:
Once Cybele, the mountain Mother of the Gods,
With driving feet
Rushed up the wooded ravines
And racing rivers,
Resounding salty waves,   1305
In longing for her captured daughter,
Whose name cannot be spoken.
The thundering cymbals cast
Their roar and blared out,
When the goddess yoked   1310
Her chariot to beasts
[To track] her daughter,
Snatched from the circling
Choirs of virgins.
As swift-footed as storms,
Artemis with her bow and wild-eyed   1315
Athena with her spear and armor
[Darted to save her.] From the bright heavens,
Zeus devised another fate.

When Cybele had stopped her wandering days,
Her driving grief,   1320
Seeking her daughter's insane
And treacherous ravisher,
She reached the peaks of Ida,
That nourish snow, a tower for nymphs,

Helen | 145

And flung herself in sorrow   1325
To snow-deep rocks and trees.
For men, the plains withered.
She made fruitless the fields
And blighted a generation.
She gave the herds no   1330
Fresh feed or leaves.
Life left the cities.
No sacrifices were offered.
Offerings lay on the altars unburnt.
She stopped the tender springs from pouring   1335
Out their bright white waters, in grief
For her daughter, taking vengeance.

After she ended the feasting
Of gods and mankind,
Zeus, trying to calm
The Mother's Stygian hate, called out: 1340
"Go down, O holy Graces,
Go, and with your ecstatic cries,
Banish Deo's pain,
Furious for her daughter.
Go, too, Muses, with your choral songs."   1345
For the first time, Aphrodite,
Most beautiful of the blessed,
Took up the quaking clash of bronze and drums
With stretched hides. Cybele laughed,
Received into her hands   1350
The thunderous pipe,
Rejoicing in its roar.

Neither right nor holy
Was what you burned,
Helen, in caverns.   1355

You won the hate of the Great Mother,
Dishonoring her rites.
Know great power lies in dappled fawn skin
Clothes, and greenery,
Ivy that crowns the sacred   1360
Thyrsus, whirly shaking high in air
Of the bull-roar's circling wood,
Hair streaming in the dance and wild
For Bromius in bacchic ritual,
In night-long rites for the goddess.   1365
The moon surpassed her well
In light, but you
Admired your own beauty.

    (HELEN enters.)

HELEN:
We were fortunate inside the house, my friends.
Proteus' daughter helped to conceal   1370
My husband's presence, under questioning.
She did not tell her brother. She said, for my sake,
He was dead under earth and does not see the
       sunlight.
My husband enjoys the greatest fortune.
The weapons he was supposed to throw into the sea,   1375
Setting his noble arm in the shield strap,
He carries himself and brings a spear in his right hand,
As if to assist in the dead man's service.
He has dressed for battle work, to win,
By hand, trophies over many barbarians,   1380
When we board the well-oared ship.
Changing his clothes from his shipwreck rags,
I fitted him out and bathed his flesh,
Finally a washing in pure river water.

But since this man comes out of the palace,   1385
Thinking to have my marriage in hand,
I must be silent. We beg you
To wish us well and control your tongue.
If we can be saved, maybe we can save you, too.

(THEOCLYMENUS enters with MENELAUS and
SERVANTS.)

THEOCLYMENUS:
Come in formation, as the stranger ordered,   1390
Men, bearing the funeral gifts for the sea.
Helen, if I seem not to speak badly,
Obey, stay here. Being present, or not,
You perform these rites for your husband.
I'm afraid some desire will take   1395
You to hurl yourself into the waves,
Struck mad by your former husband's charms,
Grieving for him no longer here.

HELEN:
O my celebrated husband, I must honor
My first marriage and bridal love.   1400
Because I loved my husband,
I would have died with him. But what good
Would it do the dead man to die with him?
Let me give the funeral gifts to the corpse myself.
May the gods give you what I wish   1405
And to this stranger for helping out.
You shall have me for the wife you should have
In your house, since you do Menelaus
And me good service. All is turning out well.
Whoever will give us a ship to carry these things,   1410
Order him to, so my joy will be complete.

THEOCLYMENUS:
Go and bring a Sidonian fifty-oared galley
For them and skilled rowers.

HELEN:
Will not the arranger of the burial command the
        ship?

THEOCLYMENUS:
Of course. My sailors must obey him.   1415

HELEN:
Order again so they understand you clearly.

THEOCLYMENUS:
I order again, even three times, if you want.

HELEN:
Thank you. May I benefit from my plans.

THEOCLYMENUS:
Don't ruin your complexion too much with tears.

HELEN:
Today will show you my gratitude.   1420

THEOCLYMENUS:
Trouble taken for the dead is useless suffering.

HELEN:
Those things I speak of matter, here, *and* there.

THEOCLYMENUS:
You shall have a husband no worse than Menelaus.

HELEN:
You are flawless. I need only good fortune.

THEOCLYMENUS:
It's yours—if you give me your good will.   1425

HELEN:
I won't be taught now how to love my loved ones.

THEOCLYMENUS:
Want me to help by bringing the expedition myself?

HELEN:
Oh no. Don't be a slave to your slaves, my lord.

THEOCLYMENUS:
All right, then. I forego the customs of Pelops' sons.
My palace is pure, for Menelaus   1430
Did not give up his soul here. Let someone go
Tell my staff to bring the wedding images
Into my palace. The whole country
Must resound with blessed hymns,
So the marriage of Helen and me may be envied.   1435

Go into the arms of the sea and give
These things to her former husband.
Hurry back my wife to my palace
And share the wedding feast with me,
So you may set out for home, or remain here happy.   1440

          (THEOCLYMENUS exits.)

MENELAUS:
O Zeus, celebrated as father and wise god,

Look upon us and set aside our suffering.
Eagerly help us haul our misfortunes to the rocky height.
But touch us with your fingertip,
We'll arrive at the good fortune we want.   1445
We struggled with enough troubles in the past.
You were called before, you gods, to hear my great
And unheeded pain. I should not fare badly always,
But go the right way. Give me one favor
And set me in good fortune forever.   1450

(MENELAUS, HELEN, and SERVANTS exit.)

CHORUS:
O swift Phoenician ship
Of Sidon, rowing, dear
To the waves of Nereus,
Leading choreographed dances
Of the dolphins, when the sea   1455
Is without a breeze,
And gray-eyed Pontus' daughter
Galineia says:
"Let the sails hang down.
Forget the ocean winds.   1460
Take up your oars of fir,
O sailors, sailors,
Bringing Helen
To the well-harbored shores of Perseus' home."

Then, Helen, you might find   1465
The daughters of Leucippus
By the river waves of Pallas'
Temple, joining at last
Choruses or revels, night
Joys of Hyacinthus   1470

Helen

Whom Phoebus killed in the contest,
Hurling far the discus.
In the Spartan land,
That son of Zeus proclaimed
A day of sacrifice.   1475
The child you left home,
[Helen, greet]
Where the pine torches are not yet fired for her wedding.

Would that we might fly
Through air where Libyan
Cranes in formation will go,   1480
Leaving the winter rains,
Obedient to the oldest,
With his shepherd-like piping,
Who shrills as he flies over
The rainless plains   1485
And fertile lands.
Flocking with the racing clouds,
O long-neck birds,
Fly midway beneath the Pleiades
And Orion by night,   1490
Herald the news,
By the Eurotas,
That Menelaus took the city
Of Troy and shall come home.

Would that you might come   1495
Through air and ride down
Sky-tracks, O sons of Tyndareus,
Dwelling in heaven beneath
The shifting, flaming stars,
You twin saviors of Helen.   1500
Upon the green salt surge,

The thrashing waves,
And dark-gray sea,
Sending favoring gusts of winds,
From Zeus to sailors,   1505
Cast off the disgrace of a barbarian
Bed from Helen, your sister,
Punished for strife
Upon Mount Ida
Who never went to Troy at all,   1510
To towers built by Phoebus.

(THEOCLYMENUS enters followed by a MESSENGER.)

MESSENGER:
My lord, I've discovered the worst for our house.
Strange the misery you'll soon hear from me.

THEOCLYMENUS:
What is it?

MESSENGER:
                    Woo another woman.
Helen's gone from the land.   1515

THEOCLYMENUS:
Taken by wings or treading feet?

MESSENGER:
Menelaus sailed off with her,
Who came himself announcing he had died.

THEOCLYMENUS:
A terrible message! What ship
Took her out of the country? I don't believe it.   1520

MESSENGER:
The one you gave the foreigner. He went
And took your sailors. That's the story.

THEOCLYMENUS:
How? I must know. I never thought
One man would overpower
The many sailors you brought.   1525

MESSENGER:
After she left the royal palace,
Zeus' daughter set out for the sea.
Turning a graceful foot, she lamented with great skill.
Her husband was at her side—and not dead.

When we came to the dockyard enclosure,   1530
We started to launch the new Sidonian ship,
Fitted out for fifty benches and oars,
One task followed another. One man
Laid down the mast. Another the oars. Another
The oars arranged for hands. The white sails   1535
Were placed. The rudders let down by ropes.

During this work, the Greek men,
Menelaus' shipmates, dressed in shipwreck rags,
Handsome men but filthy to see,
Were on the lookout for this and came to the shore.   1540
Seeing them there, the son of Atreus, bringing
Out his treacherous lament, addressed them:
"Poor wretches, how and from what Greek boat
Do you come, shattering your ship?
Help us bury the destroyed son of Atreus,   1545
Whom Tyndareus' daughter honors with a cenotaph,
He being far from here." They wept false tears

And went into the ship carrying offerings
For Menelaus. We were suspicious and spoke
To each other of the great number   1550
Of additional passengers. Nevertheless we obeyed
Your commands. By ordering the stranger
To run the ship, you ruined everything.

We set the rest, being light, in the ship easily.
But the bull did not want to set his foot   1555
Straight forward along the gangway.
He bellowed out, rolling his eyes,
Arching his back, and looking along his horn,
Keeping us from touching him. Helen's husband
called, "O sackers of Troy city, come   1560
Won't you lift the bull's bulk, according
To Greek custom, on your sturdy shoulders
And heave him into the prow"—he took his sword
In his hand—"a sacrifice for the dead man?"
At his order, they came and hove up the bull,   1565
Carried it, and set it on the deck.
Patting the neck and forehead of the horse,
Menelaus persuaded it to enter the ship.

Finally, when the boat was full,
After gracing the ladder with her beautiful ankles,   1570
Helen sat in the middle of the quarterdeck—
And he who was dead only in words.
Others sat in pairs, equally
Starboard and port, holding swords
Concealed beneath their cloaks, and the waves filled   1575
With our voices echoing the boatswain's calls.

When we were not too far from the land,
Or too near, the helmsman asked,

"Still farther, stranger? Is this good?
Shall we row on? You're in charge."   1580
He answered, "Far enough." Seizing his sword,
He walked to the prow and stood by the sacrificial
Bull. Making no mention of the dead,
He cut the throat and prayed, "O Poseidon,
Dwelling in the sea, and Nereus' holy daughters,   1585
Bring me and my wife to Nauplia's shores,
Safe out of this land." Streams of blood spouted
Into the waves propitiously for the stranger.

Someone said, "There's treachery aboard.
Let's sail back. Order us to starboard!
Turn the rudder!" Standing at the dead bull,   1590
Atreus' son shouted to his shipmates,
"Why do you hesitate, flower of Greece,
To slaughter, murder the barbarians and toss
Them from the ship to the waves?" The boatswain   1595
Called the opposite command to your sailors:
"Come on! Will someone not take up a spar for a spear;
Another shatter the benches; someone rip the oar
From its pin; and bloody the heads of the warring
         strangers?"
All sprang up. These holding ship's   1600
Spars in their hands; those swords.
The ship flowed with blood. From the stern,
Helen urged them on: "Where is your Trojan glory?
Show it to the barbarians." In battle heat
They fell. Some rose up. You could see   1605
Others lying dead. Menelaus in arms,
Spying where his men were harassed,
Pressed on with his sword in his right hand.
So your men dove overboard. He cleared
The oar seats of your sailors. He went   1610

To the helmsman and told him to steer to Greece.
They stepped the mast. Favorable winds came.

They went from the country. To escape death,
I let myself down by the anchor into the sea.
A fisherman picked me up exhausted   1615
And put me on shore to announce
The news to you. There is nothing more useful
To mortals than prudent distrust.

CHORUS:
My lord, I wouldn't have expected Menelaus
To escape your notice and mine, right here.   1620

THEOCLYMENUS:
O miserable me, taken in by female treachery.
My bride has escaped me. If the ship could be overtaken,
I would make every effort to take the foreigners.
Now I shall punish my betrayer of a sister,
She, seeing Menelaus in the palace, didn't tell me.   1625
She won't delude another man with her prophecies.

CHORUS LEADER:
You, where are you rushing, my lord, to what murder?

THEOCLYMENUS:
Where justice calls me. Move out of the way!

CHORUS LEADER:
I shall not let go of your robe. You're heading for great
    trouble.

THEOCLYMENUS:
What! A slave, you rule your master?

Helen | 157

CHORUS LEADER:

               I know best.   1630

THEOCLYMENUS:
Not for me, if you don't let me . . .

CHORUS LEADER:

             —No, I won't let you—

THEOCLYMENUS:
Kill a most vile sister . . .

CHORUS LEADER:

          —No, the holiest of all—

THEOCLYMENUS:
Who betrayed me . . .

CHORUS LEADER:

        —beautiful betrayal, doing justice—

THEOCLYMENUS:
Giving my bride to another . . .

CHORUS LEADER:

           —to her more rightful
              guardian.—

THEOCLYMENUS:
Who *is* the guardian of my property?

CHORUS LEADER:

            He who took her from
              her father.   1635

THEOCLYMENUS:
Chance gave her to me . . .

CHORUS LEADER:
and necessity took her away.

THEOCLYMENUS:
It is not right that you judge mine.

CHORUS LEADER:
It is if I speak better.

THEOCLYMENUS:
I'm ruled then, not the ruler.

CHORUS LEADER:
Ruler to do right, not what is
unjust.

THEOCLYMENUS:
You seem to love death.

CHORUS LEADER:
Kill me. You won't kill
Your sister, if I can help it. It is a most glorious death   1640
For a noble slave to die for his mistress.

(The Dioscuri, CASTOR and POLYDEUCES, enter
above on the theater crane.)

CASTOR:
Cease your anger. You've gone wrong,
Theoclymenus, lord of the land. We, the two
Dioscuri, call, whom Leda bore

With Helen, who has fled your palace.   1645
You are angry about a marriage not destined for you.
Nor was the daughter of the Nereid goddess,
Your sister, Theonoe, unjust to you. She honored
The gods' will and her father's just commands.

It was fated that woman dwell continually   1650
In your palace until the present time.
But no more, since Troy's foundations are thrown
Down and her name belongs to the gods.
She must be reunited in the same marriage,
Go home, and live with her husband.   1655

But keep your black sword from
Your sister. Know she acted wisely.
Long ago, we might have rescued Helen,
Since Zeus had made us gods,
Though less than fate and other gods,   1660
To whom these things seemed right.

I announce this to you my sister: Sail
With your husband. You'll have favorable winds.
We, your saviors, your twin brothers,
Riding along the sea, will bring you home.   1665
When you have finished life's course and reached
       the end,
You will be called a goddess [and share libations
With the Dioscuri] and shall have feasts
From men with us. Zeus wills it so.

Where Maia's son first set you down,   1670
Taking you from Sparta in his heavenly course,
Stealing your body, lest Paris marry you,
I mean the guardian island stretched along Attica,

It will be called "Helen" forever among mortals,
Because it received you, stolen from home,   1675

For the wandering Menelaus, it is fated,
By the gods to live in the Islands of the Blest,
For the gods do not hate the wellborn,
And their pain is more than that of common men.

THEOCLYMENUS:
O sons of Leda and Zeus, I put aside   1680
My former quarrel with your sister.
Let her go home, if it is decreed by the gods.
No longer shall I try to kill Theonoe.
Know that you were born of the same blood
To a matchless and most chaste sister.   1685
Rejoice in Helen's most noble soul—
Something not found in many women.

CHORUS:
The gods take many forms.
Many things the gods bring about unexpectedly.
What is expected is not accomplished.   1690
Gods discover unexpected ways.
So it turned out here.

        (All exit.)

Notes

1–63. Prologue (what precedes the introduction of the chorus. Aristotle,
Poetics, 1452b19–20). 1–68. Helen's song (monody).

   1. *Virgin. Kalliparthenoi*, "with beautiful virgins" or "pure," stresses one

of the romance themes of the play: that Helen, unlike her phantom self who went to Troy with Paris, is still "virginal," in the sense of "pure," for Menelaus. Cf. lines 48, 59, 65, 794–801.

3. We now know that the flooding of the Nile was from heavy Ethiopian rains, not melting snow. Today dams control the water.

4. *Proteus*. The Old Man of the Sea, a shapeshifter and personification of nature (*Odyssey* 4.456–458). This magical figure prepares us for the story of the magical tale of Helen's journey and her double, as does the setting in faraway Egypt and the invocation of Homer's more romantic epic.

5. *Pharos*. A rocky island, north of Egypt.

9–10. The lines are thought partly spurious. Theoclymenus, "god-famed," is the name of a seer in the *Odyssey*.

13. *Theonoe*. "She knows the things of the gods." An idea essential for the plot.

16–48. Helen's need to explain the alternate story to the audience implies that Stesichorus' version was less well known than Homer's version. See the introduction. Note that the pursuit of beauty is a theme in this play as well as in the original tale and, in a wider sense, throughout ancient Greek culture. Helen also reveals doubts about tales of the gods.

41. *mightiest man in Greece*. Achilles.

44. *Hermes*. The messenger god.

65. Suppliancy tries to balance heroic force in the Greek world and has the support of Zeus *Heketesios* ("Of the Suppliants") (Adkins, *Merit*, 65, 80).

68. *Teucer*. Rejected by his father for not avenging the death of his brother, Ajax, at Troy, Teucer is searching for a new home, a variation of the return story (*nostos*) of Menelaus and of Odysseus.

69. *Plutus*. God of wealth.

83–142. The dialogue shifts from verse paragraphs to an exchange of one-liners (stichomythia) that heightens the drama.

99. Euripides is the first to mention that Achilles was Helen's suitor once.

109. *Phrygians*. Trojans.

110. *Achaeans*. Greeks.

124. That is, "Neither in the territory of Sparta nor in Sparta itself, where the Eurotas flows."

128. The gods punished the Greeks for atrocities at Troy by scattering the returning fleet with a storm (e.g., *Trojan Women*, 78–85).

137. *Tyndareus' sons*. The Dioscuri, Castor and Polydeuces, divine brothers of Helen. Both appear at the end of the play, though only Castor speaks.

164–252. Parodos. Entrance of the Chorus. 167–178: Strophe A. 179–190: Antistrophe A. 191–210: Strophe B. 211–228: Antistrophe B. 229–251: Epode. Teucer's situation and news of Troy's fall and aftermath stir Helen to call upon underworld goddesses for inspiration for her lament, while the chorus feared Helen was being raped by Theoclymenus. Helen and the chorus shift the plane of the action to backstory, intensifying the atmosphere of menace at the opening of the play.

169. *Sirens*. Death goddesses, whose mermaid song lures mariners away from their missions (*Odyssey* 12.39–46). Also earthly companions of Persephone (see below) who were changed into rocks in the sea, hence their plangent song.

175. *Persephone*. Carried off by Hades, Persephone (Proserpina) became a goddess of the underworld. Cf. Helen's abduction and later deification. This reference is expanded in 1301–1352.

190. *Pan*. God of flocks and shepherds and nature itself.

228. *bronze-housed goddess*. Athena. She had a temple of bronze on the acropolis in Sparta.

229–232. The war originated with Paris' voyage to Sparta. The cutting down of trees to build ships is often seen as the beginning of war, and hence evil (cf. *Iliad* 5.63). The pine sap oozes like tears for the destruction the tree will bring to Troy.

239. *Danaans*. Greeks.

244. *Son of Maia*. Hermes.

253–514. First Episode.

262. An old tradition claims that Euripides was once a painter (Barlow, *Imagery*, 15).

264–266. As a shame culture, rather than a guilt culture, the heroic world cultivated reputation.

276. The play invokes the Homeric world for an audience in the later world of the city-state (polis). The urban democratic antipathy to monarchy is evident here.

283. *My daughter*. Hermione, daughter of Helen and Menelaus.

295. *barbarian*. Ancient Greeks saw themselves as superior to other races, like the Medes and Persians, who were considered "barbarians," "speaking gibberish" ("bar"-"bar"-ians).

330–385. Lyric interlude between Helen and chorus.

349. *Eurotas*. River near Sparta.

369. *Scamander*. River near Troy.

375–380. *Callisto*. Callisto ("most beautiful") was seduced by Zeus and transformed into a bear, hence losing human consciousness. She is the constellation the Great Bear (Big Dipper). The theme of sexuality and violation continues.

381. *Artemis*. Goddess of chastity and the hunt.

382. *Merops' Titan daughter*. Cos? If so, the Aegean island bears her name.

386–387. *Pelops. Oenomaus*. Pelops was the grandfather of Menelaus and Agamemnon. At *Pisa* (near Olympia), he beat Oenomaus in a chariot race by bribing and won Hippodamia, his daughter, for his bride. Pelops' father, Tantalus, boiled him, cut him up, and fed him to the gods to test their omniscience. He was later restored to life. The Peloponessus, "Pelops' island," is named after him.

421–424. Euripides' lowering of Homeric heroes by introducing them in rags is mocked by Aeschylus, tragedian of the high style, in Aristophanes' *Frogs* (841–842). Euripides' more sophisticated urban audience is capable of a less admiring attitude toward the heroic age. Note the humorous elements in the scene later between Theoclymenus' doorkeeper and Menelaus, as well as the somewhat bombastic swagger of Menelaus here, revealing a defensive hero. In Egypt, as in classical Athens, Menelaus' stature has been somewhat reduced. As we know, and he does not, he has also been duped by Hera. The mistaken identity theme is a standard comic device. One can hardly imagine Homer's Menelaus in this scene.

474. *Lacedaemon*. Sparta.

515–527. Epiparodos: Reentry of the chorus. A highly variable astrophic lyric that momentarily lessens the tension.

528–1106. Second Episode.

544. *bacchante*. Ecstatic follower of Dionysos.

569–570. *Hecate*. An earth goddess associated with death, the underworld, and demons. She was blended with Enodia, mentioned in the Greek text by Helen, a goddess of crossroads and dreams. More phantoms.

625–697. A lyric duet (*amoibaion*) in which Menelaus' lines mostly follow the conversational iambic trimeters of the dialogue, but Helen's often veer into contrasting lyric meters (iambic and the ecstatic dochmiac, $\smile$— — $\smile$—).

658–659. *Idaean/City*. Troy, near Mount Ida.

680–681. The lines are "dropped" or split between the actors for a change in rhythm (*antilabé*).

713–719. Conventional wisdom. The unreliability of fate and the gods suggests a doubtful outcome for the play. Cf. lines 745–757. Note Euripides' sympathy for slaves as well as women.

749. *Calchas*. Greek seer.

751. *Helenus*. Trojan seer and son of Priam.

767. *Nauplius*. Nauplius' son, Palamedes, exposed Odysseus' ruse of madness to avoid going to the Trojan War and was killed by the Greeks in a plot laid by Odysseus. After a storm scattered the Greek fleet returning to Greece, Nauplius got vengeance by lighting false beacons on *Euboea* and wrecked Greek ships (in the *Cypria*). See line 128 and its note.

769. *The lookout of Perseus*. Western end of the Nile delta where the hero Perseus rescued Andromeda from a sea monster.

821. *Theonoe* = "she knows the things of the gods." Cf. note to 13.

849. Nestor. Old hero in the *Iliad*.

894–943. A rhesis (set speech) reminiscent of law courts. Poetry and oratory were closely connected in ancient Greece.

1107–1164. First Stasimon (Choral Ode). 1107–1121: Strophe A. 1122–1136: Antistrophe A. 1137–1150: Strophe B. 1151–1164: Antistrophe B. The chorus broadens the action with mythological and historical referents outside the play itself.

1110. *nightingale*. Philomela was raped by Tereus, the husband of her sister, Procne. Tereus cut out her tongue and imprisoned her in the wilds of Thrace, but she wove a tapestry of what happened and sent it to Procne. Procne killed her child, Itys, and fed him to his father Tereus. When Tereus pursued the women, the gods changed them into birds: Tereus became a hawk, Procne a swallow, and Philomela a nightingale. There are slightly variant versions of the tale. The nightingale's cry is a high-pitched frenzy followed by a long, low lamenting note, imitative of the violence and its aftermath. Such references keep the threat of rape in the mind of the audience and also the serious consequences if Helen's plan fails.

1126. *Nauplius*. See note to 767.

1165–1300. Third Episode.

1201. The first of several double entendres, e.g., 1205, 1215, 1225.

1301–1368. Second Stasimon. 1301–1318: Strophe A. 1319–1337: Antistrophe B. 1338–1352: Strophe B. 1353–1368: Antistrophe B. The kidnapped Helen invokes the tale of Persephone again (cf. note to 175).

1301-1368. The "Mountain Mother Ode." Cybele, the Great Mother, is blended here with Demeter (Deo) as the mother of Persephone, carried off by Hades to the underworld. In revenge, she neglects the crops she cares for and mankind starves. To console her, she is given the flute and joins in the blended rites of Dionysos and Aphrodite.

1312. Line corrupt. Conjecture added.

1317. Line corrupt. Conjecture added.

1340. *Stygian.* Hellish.

1341. *Graces.* Charites, goddesses of poetry and song, often associated with the muses.

1353-1368. The story of Helen's neglect of the rites of Cybele/Dionysos through the admiration for her own beauty is found only here, though the treatment suggests a well-known myth. Part of her misery in Egypt is the result of this neglect. Note the contrast with Cybele's acceptance of Bacchic rites (1349-1352).

1358. *fawn skin.* Worn by the followers of Dionysos.

1360-1361. *Thyrsus.* The fennel reed stuffed with *Ivy* at the top, carried by Dionysos' bacchants as a wand.

1362. *the bull-roar's circling wood.* The rhombus, a cult instrument of wood, whirled on a string to make a frightening roar.

1364. *Bromius.* Dionysos, the "roaring" god.

1366-1368. Highly disputed lines.

1369-1450. Fourth Episode.

1412. *Sidonian.* A city in Phoenicia, Sidon, constructed the best ships.

1451-1511. Third Stasimon. 1451-1464: Strophe A. 1465-1477: Antistrophe A. 1478-1494: Strophe B. 1495-1511: Antistrophe B. Perhaps inspired by Helen's suggestion that the Greek women too might return to Greece (1389), the chorus foresees and celebrates the voyage of Helen and Menelaus and themselves to Greece.

1457. *Galineia.* = "Calm." A sea goddess.

1464. *Perseus' home.* Perseus founded Mycenae, near Sparta.

1466. *The daughters of Leucippus.* Phoebe and Hilaeira. The wives of the Dioscuri, Castor and Polydeuces. Euripides invokes the cult of the Leucippides in Sparta that was like that of Helen.

1467. *Pallas.'* Athena's.

1470. *Hyacinthus.* A boy loved by Apollo (*Phoebus* [1471]) but accidently killed by him in a discus throw. The object of a Spartan cult.

1477. Lacuna and conjecture.

1497. *sons of Tyndareus*. The Dioscuri, Castor and Polydeuces, who appear shortly in the play.

1512–1692. Exodos.

1512–1618. As often, a messenger arrives to fill in the action offstage and to offer another point of view from the characters or the chorus. In this case it is a soldier, who changes the tone to Homeric epic, while at the same time criticizing Theoclymenus' actions.

1535. Text uncertain at beginning of the line.

1541. *son of Atreus*. Menelaus.

1556–1566. The bull's recalcitrance is an evil omen for the sailor/narrator.

1586. *Nauplia's shores*. Port near Sparta.

1621–1641. Shift to (double) Greek trochaic tetrameters. — ◡ — ◡ — ◡ — ◡ — ◡ — ◡ — ◡. Longer lines. Falling rhythm.

1630–1639. More *antilabé*, or "dropped" lines.

1642. The deus ex machina (god from a machine—i.e., the crane) that enters the play has given us the literary term to ending a play externally. In this case, the Dioscuri carry out the will of the gods and the insights of Theonoe, though Helen and Menelaus had to work out the means of their delivery themselves, a combination of Odyssean trickery and Achillean force.

1667–1668. Partly spurious lines.

1673–1674. The island now called Makronissos was named Helen. (Cf. introduction.)

1688–1692. The play ends with a sense that benevolent gods provide for us in the world. But the final choral song says, as often, only that the gods bring about the unexpected. But what about the Greek women of the chorus left in Egypt (cf. line 1389)? Do we assume their return? And what of other plays of Euripides. *Trojan Women*? *Hecuba*? The gods interfere with human life, saving some, destroying others.

HECUBA

Introduction

Vengeance is mine; I will repay, saith the Lord
Romans 12:19

Revenge triumphs over death
Francis Bacon, "Of Death"

Literature and law have often been at odds over the concept of revenge. Indeed, revenge is a crux within the field of law, too. Often families feel that the idea of punishment only as a deterrent does not bring justice, while law usually holds that punishment belongs to the state. Recently, a father in Texas beat a rapist to death on the spot for attacking his nine-year-old daughter. He was not even charged, for no jury would convict him. In ancient Greece, revenge was still more acceptable, sometimes even a duty (Mossman, *Wild Justice*, 169). Literature has frequently presented, and sometimes satisfied, this thirst for blood vengeance, from Achilles' revenge against his Greek allies and Odysseus' slaughter of the suitors, to *Hamlet* and to films like *Taxi Driver*. While Aeschylus' *Oresteia* commemorated a shift from heroic revenge to law, breaking the circle of vengeance, Euripides, in his *Medea* and *Hecuba*, continued to dramatize and complicate the act of revenge. These and other Greek revenge plays influenced Shakespeare and many others. Often, as in Euripides, it is women who turn to blood law (McHardy, *Revenge*, 37–42). Even today.

As victim, Hecuba is the *mater dolorosa* of classical literature, but, in this play, she turns into *la mère sauvage* of unmitigated violence in a subtle and forceful tragedy that examines deeply the roots of hatred and revenge. Hecuba's city was destroyed after her son, Paris, carried off Helen from Sparta to Troy. Ten years of war led to Odysseus' ruse of the wooden horse, the slaughter of the Trojan men, and the enslavement of the women

Hecuba

and children. Hecuba survives the deaths of her husband, children, and city, to suffer on the Greek stage in this play that bears her name and in *Trojan Women*. The two plays represent the passive and active sides of her ordeal. In *Hecuba*, she loses her daughter Polyxena, and discovers her dead son Polydorus. The army kills Polyxena, but a tyrant, Polymestor, kills her son, and Hecuba plots revenge. Her passive suffering in the play drives her active revenge in the second half and perhaps her degeneration into the mad dog she becomes in legend (cf. Cicero, *Tusculan Disputations*, 3.63.13).The story is set in Homeric times but is viewed by Greeks of the later city-state. Her revenge presents a dilemma to the audience: Is her revenge justified? Does she go too far? Euripidean characters often go too far (e.g., Dionysos in the *Bacchae* and Medea). Euripides stirs up in his audience the desire for revenge at the same time that he questions its validity from a more modern point of view. Ultimately, the viewer must decide—or not.

For some critics, the diptych structure of the play is problematic, showing the degeneration of the Hecuba from the first half of the play. (For various reactions and references, see the Gregory edition, xxxii–xxxiiii.) We must keep in mind that excessive revenge is part of literary legend, as well as ancient and modern psychology and of the victim/avenger plot itself. As in the *Hecuba*, the violent myth of Philomela, the nightingale, also takes place in Thrace, a similarity that perhaps suggests to Hecuba her comparison of her daughter's pending atrocity to Philomela's (338). In the myth, Tereus, King of Thrace, rapes his sister-in-law, Philomela, cuts out her tongue, and walls her up in a castle in the wilderness. She weaves a tapestry, exposing Tereus' crime, and sends it to her sister, Procne. Procne, Tereus' wife, kills her and Tereus' child, Itys, and feeds him to her husband and reveals to him her revenge. Tereus pursues the two women, but the gods transform them into birds: Tereus into the first hawk, Procne into the first swallow, and Philomela into the first nightingale (the species varies a little in different versions). The myth has the archetypal pattern of victim (or victims) and excessive revenge, as in this play, as in Medea's revenge on Jason, Atreus' revenge on Thyestes, and Dionysos' revenge on Pentheus. Later renditions of the betrayal of Polydorus occur in Vergil, *Aeneid* (3.22–68), and Ovid, *Metamorphoses* (13.439–575).

Hecuba was perhaps performed in 424 BC. Athens' reestablishment of the Delian festivals in 426 may be referred to in the play (458–465) and helps to date the *Hecuba*. The Polyxena story may have come from a lost *Polyxena* by Sophocles, as an ancient scholiast tells us in his commentary on the first line. The tale also appears in *Sack of Troy* in the Epic Cycle, and in poems by Ibycus, Simonides, and Stesichorus. In these sources, Achilles' ghost demands the sacrifice of Polyxena. The second part of the play, Hecuba's revenge and "trial," could have its source in Thracian legend or be the creation of Euripides himself.

The drama occurs in Thrace, near the Hellespont, for Greeks a barbarian and barbarous land at a time when there was no law court, and random murder, rape, and outrage were the inevitable outcome of the long Trojan War. The setting and situation challenge Greek and human values. Achilles' ghost demands the sacrifice of Polyxena for what he has done in battle for the Greeks. Hecuba asks Odysseus to save her because he owes her a favor for saving his life during the war. Odysseus refuses. Polyxena replies that death is better than the slavery she faces. Polymestor violates the sacred bond of host and guest when he kills the young Polydorus for the gold he carries. Priam had sent his son away to save him from the war and carry on his line. Agamemnon must judge the case between Hecuba and Polymestor and admits its difficulty. What are valid bonds and claims? A desperate mother turns to excessive revenge. What values are just and what values remain when society is destroyed? The play ends with Agamemnon's sigh of understated relief at leaving this vexed case to return to the ease of Greek civilization:

Already I see the winds leading home.
May we have good sailing and see happily
Our homes, setting aside this trouble. (1290–1292)

Do the favoring winds suggest the approval of the gods for Hecuba's actions (Gregory edition, xxi)?

A series of images of falling reinforces the action. Falling is hardly an unusual image in Greek literature, but here falling is extended in more complex, consistent, and climactic ways. The ghost of Polydorus speaks of "falling" (50) into his mother's arms when she discovers the body. When Hecuba enters, she is visibly on the verge of toppling like her city, queen of a fallen kingdom. She says of herself:

Bring the old lady, my friends, out front.
Bring and prop up your fellow slave,
Trojan women, before you—a queen!
Grasp, carry, send, raise,
Grab my old hand, too.
Leaning on the curved staff
Of your arm, I shall speed my slow steps
Setting one foot before the other. (60–67)

She does not collapse but falls deliberately at Odysseus' knees in supplication and asks her daughter Polyxena to do the same (339), but she refuses. Odysseus threatens to drag Polyxena off, and Polyxena pleads with her aged mother not to let herself be thrown down (405–406). Hecuba finally falls in a faint (439–443). In contrast, Talthybius, who comes and raises up

Hecuba, relates that the dying Polyxena threw herself on Achilles' tomb, chastely covering herself (569–570).

The chorus sings that Paris cut down the pine (made into a ship to carry off Helen and bring down Troy) (631–632). Then the fallen body of Polydorus is brought in. Hecuba exclaims:

Disaster falls upon disaster. (690)

She then contemplates falling again as a suppliant, this time at the feet of Agamemnon (737–738). She finally resolves to do it (752–753). Unlike in the former scene with Odysseus, she asks not for mercy but for revenge. The chorus sings a song of the fall of Troy (901–951). Then Hecuba, the personification of the fallen city, tells Polymestor that she is ashamed to be seen "fallen in this misfortune" (971). The chorus assures Polymestor:

Like someone falling into a harborless sea,
You shall fall far short of your heart's desire. (1025–1026)

These images culminate in the ruined Polymestor's entrance like an animal, thrown down from human status, to all fours. It is not Hecuba who totters now. She has grown strong with the satisfactions of her revenge. But Polymestor is *in extremis*:

What torture! Where go? Where stand? Where put in?
Shall I take the way of a four-foot beast
Of the mountains, on my hands tracking some quarry,
This way, turning that way,
Longing to take the man-murdering Trojan women.
    (1057–1061)

Polymestor counters that Hecuba will fall, too, in the form of a dog from a ships' mast to her death (1261, 1265). But for

Hecuba, revenge means more to her than her fall to death, as she replies in matter-of-fact, blunt, but steadfast, words:

No matter, since you paid me back. (1274)

Note on the Greek Text

Primarily, I have followed the Oxford Classical Text of James Diggle, *Euripidis Fabulae*, I (1984). (Line numbering corresponds to Diggle's text, not to my translation.) I have also used the following editions:

G. Murray, Euripides, *Euripidis Fabulae*, I (Oxford: Oxford University Press, 1902).

W. S. Hadley, Euripides, *The Hecuba of Euripides* (Cambridge: Cambridge University Press, 1894), with commentary.

M. Tierney, Euripides, *Hecuba* (Bristol: Bristol Classical Press, 1979), with commentary.

C. Collard, Euripides, *Hecuba* (Warminster: Aris & Phillips, 1991), with commentary.

D. Kovacs, Euripides, II, *Children of Heracles, Hippolytus, Andromache, Hecuba* (Cambridge, MA: Harvard University Press, 1995).

J. Gregory, Euripides, *Hecuba* (Atlanta: Scholars Press, 1999), with commentary.

List of Characters

GHOST OF POLYDORUS, son of Hecuba
HECUBA, Queen of Troy
CHORUS of Captive Trojan Women
POLYXENA, daughter of Hecuba

ODYSSEUS, King of Ithaca
TALTHYBIUS, a herald
FEMALE SERVANT to Hecuba
AGAMEMNON, King of Mycenae
POLYMESTOR, King of Thrace
TWO SONS of Polymestor (silent parts)

(The play takes place in northern Greece in Thrace
across the Hellespont from Troy. The stage building is
the tent of Agamemnon. One side entrance leads to
the sea; the other to the rest of the Greek camp. The
GHOST OF POLYDORUS appears on the roof of the
stage building.)

GHOST OF POLYDORUS:
Leaving the depths of the dead and the gates
Of shadow, where Hades settled, far from the gods,
I, Polydorus, come, child of Hecuba, Cisseus' daughter.
My father Priam, when our Phrygian city
Was in danger of falling to the Greek spear,   5
Feared for my life and smuggled me out of Troy
To Polymestor's house in foreign Thrace
Where he cultivates the fertile Chersonean plateau
And forces his horse-loving people to rejoice in his power.
My father sent with me a cache of gold   10
So, if the walls of Troy fell,
His living children would not starve.
Because I was Priam's youngest, he transported me
Out of the country, neither to bear a shield
Nor a spear, for my arm was young.   15
While the boundary stones stayed upright
And the Trojan towers unbroken
And brother Hector triumphed with his spear,

I grew strong under my Thracian father's
Nurturing, like some young shoot—all for misery!   20

When Troy and Hector's soul were destroyed,
The family hearth uprooted, and father
Fallen before the god-built altar,
Jugular split by the bloody child of Achilles,
Then my father's friend murdered me for gold   25
And plunged me into the swell of the sea,
So he might keep the gold in his house.
I lay on the beaches and in the roiling sea,
Back and forth in the running track of the waves,
Unwept, unburied. Now I dart above Hecuba,   30
My dear mother, abandoning my body,
Floating now for the third day,
The same three days my ruined mother
Is here in the Chersonese from Troy.

In spite of their ships, the Greeks   35
Idle on the Thracian shore. Peleus' son,
Achilles, appeared above his tomb
And held back the whole army
Even those piloting the ships home.
He asked for my sister Polyxena,   40
as his own victim to honor his tomb.
And it shall be done. Nor shall he
Be without gifts from his friends. Fate
Leads my sister to death this day.
My mother shall look upon two children's   45
Corpses, mine and my wretched sister's.
To bury me and my suffering, I shall appear
Before the feet of a slave girl in the waves.
I have prayed to the powers below for a tomb

And to fall into my mother's hands.   50
The very thing that will happen.

Now I shall get out of Hecuba's way.
She walks out from Agamemnon's tent,
Fearing her dream vision of me.
—What misery!—

O mother, you who see a slave's day   55
After a king's house, how horribly you fare
As you once fared well. Some god
Wrecks you, balancing former fortune.

    (GHOST OF POLYDORUS exits.)

    (HECUBA enters.)

HECUBA:
Bring the old lady, my friends, out front.   60
Bring and prop up your fellow slave,
Trojan women, before you—a queen!
Grasp, carry, send, raise,
Grab my old hand, too.
Leaning on the curved staff   65
Of your arm, I shall speed my slow steps
Setting one foot before the other.

O lightning of Zeus, darkness of night,
Why am I shaken in the dark
By fearful phantoms? O revered Earth,   70
Mother of black-winged dreams,
I drive off a fearful apparition of the night
In which I learned in a dream about my child
Who was saved in Thrace
And my dear daughter Polyxena.   75

O deities of earth, save my child
Who, lone anchor of our house,   80
Lives in snowy Thrace
Under the guardianship of a fatherly friend.
Something new shall come to pass,
Some mournful song for those in mourning.
Never has my heart so relentlessly   85
Shivered, so feared.
Where may I see the divine soul of Helenus,
My women, and see Cassandra,
So they may interpret my dreams?

I saw in the bloody maw of a wolf a spotted deer   90
Slaughtered, snatched from my knees.
And this further terror:
Above the top of his tomb came
The ghost of the head of Achilles. He asked
For some present from the suffering Trojans.   95
Gods, send this ghost away, far far away
From my child, I beg you.

            (CHORUS enters.)

CHORUS:
Hecuba, I have slipped out to you quickly
Leaving my master's tent,
Forced there as a slave   100
Driven far from the Trojan
City at spear point,
Hunted down by the Achaean spear.
I bring no relief for your sorrow,
Distraught by the weight of bad news,   105
A herald, grieving for you, lady.
It is said to be decreed in the full assembly
Of the Achaeans that your daughter

Be made a victim to Achilles. As you know
He appeared above his tomb with golden weapons   110
And held back the seafaring ships
That billowed their sails to the forestays.
He shouted out: "Where, Danaans,
Are you going without setting a gift of honor
On my tomb?"   115
Waves of great strife clashed:
Opinion split the warrior force
Of the Greeks in two: whether it seemed best
To give the tomb a victim, or not.
Urging what's right for you,   120
Agamemnon was faithful to the bed
Of your bacchic daughter Cassandra.
But the sons of Theseus, the double branches
Of Athens, both orators, spoke
And held one opinion: 125
To crown Achilles' tomb
With fresh blood, and not, they said,
To value the bed of Cassandra
Above the spear of Achilles.
Strained words held equal weight   130
On both sides, until the wily liar,
The sweet crowd-pleaser,
Son of Laertes, persuaded the army
Not to insult the best of all the Danaans
Over the mere sacrificing of a slave.   135
Nor should anyone of the wasted dead
Standing in Persephone's house say
The Danaans left the plains of Troy
Without thanking those Danaans
Who died for Greece.   140
Odysseus comes right now
To drag your child from your breasts,

To rip her from your old hands.
But go to the temples, go to the altars,
Sit suppliant at Agamemnon's knees.   145
Summon the gods both of heaven and hell.
Either your prayers will keep
You from losing your unhappy child.
Or you must look on the girl
Falling before the tomb,   150
Her throat decked in gold
And pouring out a scarlet flood.

HECUBA:
Wretched, what shall I say?
What lament, what lament can I make,   155
Rotten from rotten old age,
Unbearable slavery
Unendurable? How I'm ruined.
Who defends me? What family,
What city? My husband gone.   160
My children gone.
Do I go this way or that?
Where shall I feel safe?
Where is the god or divinity to help me?
O my Trojan women, bringers of pain,   165
Bringers of pain,
You have devastated, devastated me.
For me, life in the daylight
Holds no more pleasure.

Worn-out feet, lead, lead   170
This old woman
To this tent. O child, O daughter
Of a most unhappy mother, come,
Come out of the tent. Hear

Your mother's voice, child, so you may know   175
What, what I hear reported about your life.

    (POLYXENA enters.)

POLYXENA:
Mother, mother, what are you shouting? What news
Do you bring, scaring me from the tent
Like a frighted bird?

HECUBA:
Ah, my child!   180

POLYXENA:
Why that cry? An evil omen for me.

HECUBA:
It's for your life!

POLYXENA:
Speak out. Don't keep it from me longer.
Your lament, mother,
Terrifies me.   185

HECUBA:
Child, a miserable mother's child!

POLYXENA:
What news do you bring?

HECUBA:
By common consent, the Argives
Are determined to sacrifice you at the tomb
For Peleus' son.   190

POLYXENA:
What do you mean, mother?
Explain such sad horrors,
Mother, explain it to me!

HECUBA:
I speak cursed words, child.
By vote of the Argives, a decree   195
goes out upon your life.

POLYXENA:
Suffering all, my wretched
Mother with a star-crossed life,
What more hateful
And unspeakable outrage   200
Has some deity brought you?
I'm your child no longer,
No longer the sad sharer of your hard age,
Your fellow slave.
Like a cub reared in the mountains   205
Or calf—O, poor us—
You shall see me carried off from your hands,
My throat cut, sent down to the darkness of earth
To hell. There with the dead
I shall bed down, wretched.   210
Mother, I weep for miserable you,
In all-out lament.
I don't weep for my life,
An outrage and a ruin.
My death is the better fortune.   215

CHORUS:
Odysseus comes here in haste, Hecuba,
Signaling some news for you.

Hecuba | 183

(ODYSSEUS enters.)

ODYSSEUS:
Woman, I think you know the army's verdict
And the vote cast. However, I shall tell you:
It was decreed by the Achaeans to sacrifice your daughter,   220
Polyxena, at the tall mound of Achilles' tomb.
They appointed me her guide and conductor.
The son of Achilles shall preside as performer
Of the sacrifice and as priest. You know
What's to be done. Don't let her be dragged by force,   225
Or you fight hand-to-hand with me.
Know your strength and how bad off you are.
You need to think wisely, even in disaster.

HECUBA:
My god! A great struggle appears here,
Full of groans and not empty of tears.   230
I did not die when I should have.
Zeus didn't destroy me but nourishes
Poor me to see greater evils still.
If a slave may question a free man,
Without insult or torturing the heart,   235
I have the right to ask,
And you to listen to my questions.

ODYSSEUS:
You may. Ask. I'll give you time.

HECUBA:
You know when you came as a spy to Troy,
A wreck in rags, and drops of blood   240
Trickled from your eyes?

ODYSSEUS:
Yes, it touched my heart deeply.

HECUBA:
Did Helen know you and tell me alone?

ODYSSEUS:
I remember I was in great danger.

HECUBA:
Humbly did you grasp my knees?   245

ODYSSEUS:
So much my hand went numb on your robe.

HECUBA:
What did you say, being my slave?

ODYSSEUS:
Many reasons not to die.

HECUBA:
Did I not save you and send you out of the land?

ODYSSEUS:
So I might see this sunlight.   250

HECUBA:
Have you not turned bad with this edict,
You who got from me what you say?
You do nothing good for us but all the evil you can.
Yours is a thankless generation, seeking
A demagogue's honors. Be far from me,   255

You who don't care about ruining your friends,
If you say something pleasing to the mob.

But with what wisdom did your leaders
Vote to murder this child?
The need to bring human sacrifice to the tomb   260
Where it is more fitting to kill oxen?
Or does Achilles, wishing to kill his killers,
Justly demand her death for his?
But she did him no wrong.
It is Helen he must demand for a tomb-sacrifice,   265
That woman destroyed him, brought him to Troy.
If a captive must be picked out to die
And be of superior beauty, that is not our lot.
Tydareus' daughter is the most extraordinary beauty,
A doer of evil second to none of us.   270
I challenge the justice of this case.

But hear what you must pay me back.
You say you touched my hand
And this old cheek as a suppliant.
I, in return, touch yours.   275
So I demand this favor, and *I* supplicate *you*:
Don't tear my child from my hands!
Don't kill her! Enough of killing.
I rejoice in her and forget my troubles.
She is my soul's image, making up for many things:
My city, my nurse, my cane, my leader of the way.   280
The powerful should not prevail when wrong.
Nor the lucky think they will do well always.
I was lucky once, but am no longer.
One day took all my prosperity from me.   285
I beg you by your beard, feel for me.
Go counsel the Achaean army

That killing women is wrong,
Women you didn't kill at first,
But took from altars in pity.   290
Your law about bloodletting
Is the same for free men and for slaves.
Your honor will persuade them, even if you speak poorly.
The speech of dishonorable men
And honorable men does not have equal force.   295

CHORUS:
No nature is so hard that, hearing your cries
And the dirge of your great laments,
Would not drop a tear.

ODYSSEUS:
Hecuba, be instructed and in your anger don't make
One speaking well an enemy in your heart.   300
I was fortunate then, and I am ready
To save your life. I won't say otherwise.
But what I said in front of all, I won't deny:
Troy being taken, give the army's
First man your child, the sacrifice he demands.   305
Many cities suffer for this reason:
When someone is noble and aggressive,
He gets no more than the cowards.
To us, Achilles is worthy of honor, lady,
A man who died for Greece in the most beautiful way.   310
Is it not a disgrace if we treat him as a friend
When alive and mistreat him when he is dead?
So. What will someone say if the army
Gathers again and renews the struggles
Of war? Will we fight, or hold back,   315
When we see the dead unhonored?
When I am alive, if I have little

Day to day, all would be well.
I wish to know that my tomb
Will be honored. Gratitude at last.   320

If you say you suffer miserably, listen:
We have old women and men
Far more pitiable than you,
Brides deprived of the best bridegrooms.
Mount Ida's dust covers their bodies.   325
Endure it! If we think wrongly to honor
The worthy, we deserve to be called stupid.
You barbarians don't believe friends are friends
Or admire those who died heroically.
In this, Greece is fortunate, and you get   330
What you deserve for your ideas.

CHORUS:
Oh me! Slavery, always evil by nature,
Endures what is wrong, conquered by force.

HECUBA:
O daughter, my argument about your murder
Is thrown useless to the winds.   335
And you, if you have more power at all
Than your mother, hurry and hurl all your voice
Like the nightingale's, that they take not your life.
Pitiably fall before Odysseus' knees
And persuade him. You have your plea: 340
For he has children and so may pity your fate.

POLYXENA:
I see you hiding your right hand
Under your cloak, Odysseus, and turning
Your face away so I won't touch your beard.

Be at ease. You're free from my Zeus of the Suppliants.   345
I accept the favor of necessity
And the need to die. If I wish otherwise,
I appear a coward too in love with life.
Why should I live? My father was lord
Of all Phrygia. This was my birth.   350
Then I was raised with great hopes
To be a bride for a king, to cause no small competition
In marriage for him whose house and hearth I should
        come to.
Unfortunate, I was the mistress among the Idaean
Virgins and women, gazed upon by all,   355
Equal to gods, except in death.

First I'm a slave now. The unaccustomed
Name makes me want to die.
Then, I'll get the brute heart
Of a master buying me for silver,   360
Me, the sister of Hector and many others,
Making me grind corn in their homes,
Forcing me to live wretched days,
Sweep the house, be set to weaving.
A slave bought somewhere will pollute   365
My bed, once worthy of kings.
No! I take the sunlight from my free eyes
And give my dead body to Hades.
Come, Odysseus, lead me to my end,
As for me I see no reason to hope   370
Or believe that I should ever fare well.
Mother, don't block my way
In word or deed. Encourage me to die
Before disgraceful things, unworthy of me, happen.
Who is not accustomed to experience evil,   375
Endures it, but sets his neck in the yoke with pain.

Dying is luckier than living.
Not to live nobly is to suffer greatly.

CHORUS:
Wonderful is the stamped coin of those
Born noble, and the fame of high birth   380
Increases in those who are worthy.

HECUBA:
You spoke nobly, but in that nobility
Lies the outrage. If it is necessary
To honor Peleus' son to keep free
Of blame, Odysseus, don't kill *her*.   385
Take *me* and stab me before Achilles' mound.
Don't spare me. I gave birth to Paris
Who killed Thetis' son with his bowstring.

ODYSSEUS:
Not *you*, old woman, Achilles' ghost
Asked the Achaeans to kill *her*.   390

HECUBA:
But kill me with her.
There will be twice the drink of blood
For earth and corpse that he demanded.

ODYSSEUS:
Your daughter's death is enough. No more
In addition. Would we didn't have to do *this*.   395

HECUBA:
I *must* die with my daughter!

ODYSSEUS:
What? I didn't know I had a master.

Hecuba

HECUBA:
I'll cling to her like the ivy to the oak.

ODYSSEUS:
No, if you will be persuaded by the wiser.

HECUBA:
I won't willingly give up this child.   400

ODYSSEUS:
But I won't leave here without taking her.

POLYXENA:
Mother, listen. You, son of Laertes,
Indulge an angry parent a little.
And you, poor woman, don't fight the strong.
Do you want them to throw you on the ground   405
And drag your old flesh by force,
Be shamed and torn by young arms?
You shall suffer these things. Don't! You are above it.
Dearest mother, give me your sweet hand
And lay your cheek on mine.   410
For never again, now for the last time,
I look upon the light of the sun.
You have the end of my speeches.
Mother, my source of life, I'm dying.

HECUBA:
O daughter, in the light of life, I shall slave.   415

POLYXENA:
No marriage, no marriage song: I must die.

HECUBA:
Wretched you, child, and miserable me.

POLYXENA:
I shall lie in hell without you.

HECUBA:
O, what shall I do? How end my life?

POLYXENA:
I shall die a slave from a free father.   420

HECUBA:
And I, fifty children gone!

POLYXENA:
What shall I say to Hector and your aged husband?

HECUBA:
Say I'm the most miserable of all.

POLYXENA:
O breasts, breasts that nourished me sweetly!

HECUBA:
O miserable daughter of untimely death!   425

POLYXENA:
Farewell, mother, farewell, Cassandra.

HECUBA:
Others fare well, not me.

POLYXENA:
And to my brother, Polydorus, in horse-loving Thrace.

HECUBA:
If he lives. I doubt it. I'm doomed in everything.

POLYXENA:
He lives, and shall close your dead eyes.   430

HECUBA:
I am dead from disasters, *before* I die.

POLYXENA:
Odysseus, come wrap my head in my cloak.
Before I perish, my heart has melted
In my mother's laments, and I dissolve in tears.
O sunlight, I can speak your name only   435
For the time I walk from here to
The sword and Achilles' funeral pyre.

(POLYXENA and ODYSSEUS exit.)

HECUBA:
I'm fainting. My limbs give way. My daughter,
Touch and take your mother's hand.
Don't leave me childless. I am destroyed, my friends.   440
May I see Spartan Helen, sister of the Dioscuri,
Led off like that, for with her beautiful eyes
She most shamefully captivated prosperous Troy.

CHORUS:
Breeze, ocean breeze,
Sending swift sails   445
On the swell of stagnant water, where
Will you carry wretched me?
To slave in what man's house,
A bought possession?
To the haven of a Doric land?   450
Or, to the Phthian land
Where the Apidanos, father
Of beautiful waters, makes sweet the plains?

Or island place,   455
Sending poor me
By the sweeping oars to painful rooms
Where the firstborn date palm rose
And laurel, sacred shoot,
So dear to Leto,   460
The glory of the son of Zeus?
Or with the Delian girls,
Will I praise the golden headband
And bow of the goddess Artemis?   465

Or in Athens
Embroider a saffron
robe, yoked colts,
Athena's great chariot,
In skillful weave   470
On my flowery loom,
Or, how Zeus, the son
Of Kronos put to sleep
The Titan race with double lightning?

O my children,   475
My fathers and land
Destroyed by smoke,
A smoldering spear-prize
Of the Achaeans.
I am called a slave   480
In a foreign land,
Exchange my home for Europe,
And have a bed in hell with Hades.

       (TALTHYBIUS enters.)

TALTHYBIUS:
Where would I find Hecuba, once
Queen of Ilium, Trojan women?   485

CHORUS:
This is she close by, her back to the ground,
Talthybius. She lies wrapped in her robe.

TALTHYBIUS:
O, Zeus, shall I say you watch over man,
Or possess this reputation for nothing,
Falsely seeming to be a race of gods,   490
While chance rules all in mortal affairs?
Was this not the queen of Phrygians rich in gold?
Not the wife of most prosperous Priam?
The whole city now depopulated by the spear,
And this old slave woman, childless, lies   495
Dirtying her cursed head with dust.
What sorrow! I'm an old man, like to die
Before some shameful fate trips me up.
Rise, miserable woman. From the ground
Lift your body, your all-white head.   500

HECUBA:
Leave off. Who won't allow my body
To lie here? Who are you to move me grieving?

TALTHYBIUS:
I've come, Talthybius, officer of the Danaans.
Agamemnon sent me after you, my lady.

HECUBA:
O how I love you! You come to sacrifice   505

Me on the tomb by decree of the Achaeans?
How sweet your words! Take me quickly, old man.

TALTHYBIUS:
That you may bury your dead daughter
I have come to find you. The two sons of Atreus
And the Achaean people sent me.   510

HECUBA:
What will you say? You did not come
For my death but to declare bad news?
You are destroyed, child, snatched from your mother.
To you I am childless, poor me!
How did you end her life? Decently?   515
Or did you kill her outrageously, like an enemy,
Old man? Speak those hateful words.

TALTHYBIUS:
You want me to cry twice, lady,
Out of pity for your daughter. Telling the horror,
I shall drop tears, as when she was wrecked   520
At the tomb. The whole Achaean army was there
In full by the tomb for your child's slaughter.
Achilles' son took Polyxena by the hand,
Setting her on top of the mound. I was near.
Chosen young men followed to hold down   525
With their hands the leaping of your calf.
Taking a full, solid-gold cup in his hand,
Achilles' son raised a libation
To his dead father. He signaled me
To proclaim silence to the whole Achaean army.   530
Standing beside them, I said,
"Be silent, Achaeans. Let the whole army
Be still." I calmed the multitude.

He said, "O child of Peleus, my father,
Receive my soothing libations that bring   535
Up the dead. Come and drink
The pure, dark blood of a girl, which I
And the army give you. Favor us:
Let us loosen the sterns and ships' cables
And all favorably return from Ilium   540
To come to our native land."

So he spoke, and every soldier prayed.

Then grabbing the gold-chased sword by the
        handle,
He drew it from the sheath and nodded
To the chosen young men to take the virgin.   545
When she saw this, she gave out these words:
"O Argives, sackers of my city, I die
Willingly. Let no one hold my body.
I shall give my throat with all my heart.
Kill me free before the gods,   550
As I die, a free woman. Being a princess,
I am ashamed to be called a slave among the dead."

The people roared approval, and Lord Agamemnon
Told the young men to let the virgin go.
[As soon as they heard his last word   555
Who held the highest power, they let her go.]
And when she heard the general's words,
She took the robe at the top of the shoulder
And ripped it below the ribs by the navel,
Exposing her breasts and chest as gorgeous   560
As a statue. Setting her knees on the ground
She spoke the bravest words of all.
"There, strike this, young man, if you are eager

To strike my breast. If you need to strike
Below my neck, my throat is ready."   565
And he, wishing, and unwishing, out of pity for the
      girl,
Cut her windpipe with the iron.
A spring gushed forth. Dying, she had, nevertheless,
The great foresight to fall chastely,
Hiding what should be hid from men's eyes.   570

When the breath had left the deadly sacrifice,
The Argives had different tasks.
Some sprinkled leaves with their hands
On the dead girl. Others brought pine logs
And heaped up the pyre. Anyone not bringing   575
Something heard reproaches from a carrier,
"Are you standing there, you sluggard, not having a
      robe
Or ornament in your hands for the young woman?
Why are you not giving to this great heart
And exceptional soul." I say such things about your
      dead child   580
And see that you are most blest with children
And the most cursed of women.

CHORUS:
Some horrible disaster of fate and the gods
Roils over Priam's children and my city.

HECUBA:
O daughter, I don't know what trouble to look at   585
Among so many. If I attend to one,
Another won't let me, and some other grief

Calls me, a chain of evil after evil.
And now I can't not grieve
Your calamity, wiping it from my heart.   590
But you take away much of my grief,
Proclaiming your high birth.

                           How strange,
If, by luck from the gods, bad earth bears
Good grain, and good, missing what it needs,
Yields bad fruit. But ever with men: 595
The bad are nothing other than bad,
And the noble noble, nor in misfortune
Do they corrupt their natures, but are good always.
Does birth or raising prevail?
Nevertheless, goodness can be nurtured   600
And learned well. If someone learns well, he knows
What is disgraceful by learning the standard of
        goodness.

The mind, of course, aims at these heights in vain.
Come tell this to the Argives:
Don't touch my daughter, but keep the mob   605
From her. You know the crowd of soldiers
Is unruly and sailors more anarchy
Than fire: he is a coward who does nothing evil.

        (TALTHYBIUS exits.)

        (To a FEMALE SERVANT.)

You, old woman, take a basin,
Dip it and bring seawater here,   610

So I shall wash her with her final bath,
Virginal and married in death, married
And not, and lay her out, as is right. But how?
As well as I can—What can I do?—
Collecting ornaments from the war captives   615
Who sit with me in these soldiers' quarters,
If anyone without their masters' noticing,
Has something stolen from her own home.

(FEMALE SERVANT exits.)

O glorious house! O once fortunate home!
O Priam, most wonderfully endowed   620
With children, and I this old mother of children,
How we came to nothing, robbed of our pride!
Do we ride high indeed then,
One of us acclaimed for wealthy estates,
Another honored among the citizens?   625
These are nothings. Mere structures of thought
And brags of speech. That man fares best
To whom nothing evil happens day by day.

(HECUBA exits.)

CHORUS:
Disaster had to come to me,
Misery was in store,   630
When Alexandros first cut down
Idaean pine to sail
The ocean's surge to Helen's bed.
The golden light of the sun   635
Lighted up
The most beautiful of women.

The pain and necessity, greater
than the pain, surround me.
A widespread evil from one man's folly   640
On the Simoin land,
Destruction and disaster came
From others. Strife was the shepherd's
Judgment   645
On three goddesses on Ida

And war and murder, my home in ruins.
Some Spartan girl at home laments   650
With many tears beside the fine-flowing Eurotas,
And a mother of dead children
Sets her hands to her gray hair and rakes her cheeks,   655
Bloodying her nails with her tearing.

> (FEMALE SERVANT enters with attendants carrying a
> body on a bier.)

FEMALE SERVANT:
Where is Hecuba, cursed in everything,
Conqueror of every race of man and woman
In sorrow? No one will dispute that crown.   660

CHORUS:
What is it, wretched woman with a wretched voice?
How announcements of my sorrows never sleep!

FEMALE SERVANT:
I bring Hecuba this sorrow. It is not easy
For mortal tongues to speak well in misery.

> (HECUBA enters.)

CHORUS:
She happens to be leaving her tent,   665
Appearing in time for your news.

FEMALE SERVANT:
Lady, suffering more than I can say.
Dead, you still see the light,
Childless, man-less, city-less, a ruin.

HECUBA:
You say nothing new but taunt one who knows.   670
But why do you bring me Polyxena's corpse,
Her tomb was decreed to be
The business of every Achaean hand?

FEMALE SERVANT (to herself):
She sees nothing, but laments Polyxena
To me and does not notice fresh disasters.   675

HECUBA:
Oh me! You are not bringing here
The bacchic body of the prophetess Cassandra?

FEMALE SERVANT:
She you cry for lives. You don't lament
This dead man. Look on the body stripped.
See if this marvel is beyond belief!   680

HECUBA:
O sorrow! I see my dead child, Polydorus.
The Thracian saved him for me in his home.

I am wrecked by misfortune. I am no more.
O child, O child
I start the bacchic rite.   685
Just now learned
From a demon of destruction.

FEMALE SERVANT:
You perceive your child's death, poor woman?

HECUBA:
I suffer the unbelievable, the unbelievable, the new and
         the new.
Disaster falls upon disaster.   690
No day shall ever pass
Without a tear, without a groan.

CHORUS:
We suffer, sad woman, terrible, terrible pain.

HECUBA:
O child, O child of a sad mother,
By what fate did you perish? By what destiny do you
         lie dead?   695
By what hand?

CHORUS:
I don't know. I found him on the beach.

HECUBA:
A castaway, or victim of a bloody spear
Upon the sandy shore?   700

FEMALE SERVANT:
A sea wave took him from the water.

HECUBA:
O god, my god, I understand
That dream before my eyes
—The black-winged phantom
Did not delude me—That 705
I saw about you, child,
No longer in the light of Zeus.

CHORUS:
Who killed him? Can you read the dream?

HECUBA:
My host, my host, a Thracian knight, 710
Where his old father sent him secretly.

CHORUS:
What do you mean? He killed him for gold?

HECUBA:
Unspeakable, unnamable, beyond belief,
Unholy and unbearable! Where is the justice for
the guest? 715
O most abominable of men. How you have torn
His flesh and with a sword of iron
Have slashed his limbs and had no pity on my
child. 720

CHORUS:
Miserable lady, some god sets hard
Upon you, suffering everything.
But I see the figure of Lord Agamemnon.
So let us be silent, my friends. 725

(AGAMEMNON enters.)

AGAMEMNON:
Hecuba, why do you delay to bury
Your child in the tomb? Talthybius told me
You said no Greek should touch your daughter.
We agreed and did not touch her.
You waste time, which amazes me.   730
I came to take you away. Everything is done
Well there—if such a thing can be done well.

Wait! What dead Trojan do I see
By the tent? The clothes he wears
Tell me he's no Greek.   735

HECUBA (to herself):
Wretched you—I mean myself—
Hecuba, what shall I do? Fall
At Agamemnon's knees, or bear trouble in silence?

AGAMEMNON:
Why do you cry and turn your back to my face,
And not say what happened? Who is this?   740

HECUBA:
But if he thinks I'm a slave and enemy
And shoves me away, I'll suffer.

AGAMEMNON:
I was not born a prophet, who, not
Hearing, shall divine your ways.

HECUBA:
Do I calculate more hostility   745
In this man's mind than there is?

Hecuba | 205

AGAMEMNON:
If you want me to know nothing
Of this, good. I want to hear nothing.

HECUBA:
I can't avenge my children without him.
Why am I debating this?   750
I must risk it, whether I succeed, or not.

Agamemnon, I supplicate your knees
And beard and fortunate right hand.

AGAMEMNON:
What do you need? Is it not to set
Free your life? That's easily done.   755

HECUBA:
Not at all. Avenging myself on evil men,
I would gladly slave my whole life.

AGAMEMNON:
What help do you want?

HECUBA:
Nothing that you imagine, my lord.
You see this corpse I cry for?   760

AGAMEMNON:
I do. But what it means I can't tell.

HECUBA:
I bore him once, carried him in my womb.

AGAMEMNON:
Which child is it, poor woman?

HECUBA:
Not one of Priam's sons who died at Troy.

AGAMEMNON:
You bore another son, my lady?   765

HECUBA:
For nothing, it seems. You see him.

AGAMEMNON:
Where was he when the city was destroyed?

HECUBA:
His father sent him away, dreading his death.

AGAMEMNON:
Where did he go, that single child of yours?

HECUBA:
To this country, where he was found dead.   770

AGAMEMNON:
To the man who rules this country, Polymestor?

HECUBA:
He was sent here, guardian of the cruelest gold.

AGAMEMNON:
Who, what evil fate brought his death?

HECUBA:
Who else? His Thracian host killed him.

AGAMEMNON:
The bastard, was he so in love with gold?   775

HECUBA:
Of course. When he knew the misfortune of the Trojans.

AGAMEMNON:
Where did you find him? Who brought the body?

HECUBA:
This woman, happening to be on the beach.

AGAMEMNON:
Searching for him, or laboring on her own?

HECUBA:
She went to get bathwater from the sea for Polyxena.   780

AGAMEMNON:
His host killed him, it seems, and threw him into the sea.

HECUBA:
Beaten by the sea, hacked by the sword.

AGAMEMNON:
Poor woman of immeasurable sorrow!

HECUBA:
Devastation, Agamemnon, and no misery not mine.

AGAMEMNON:
What agony! What woman born so luckless!   785

HECUBA:
None. Except Misfortune herself.
But for the reason I fall at your knees,
Listen. If I appear to suffer by divine law,
I am content. If not, be my avenger
On this most sacrilegious man and host,   790
Who, fearing no gods below or above,
Committed a most sacrilegious crime.
Often we shared a table, him first
In rank for hospitality among my guests.
So many obligations, such honor—and he kills my
            boy!   795
Beyond planning and killing him, he thought him
Unworthy of a grave and flung him into the sea.

I am a slave, and perhaps weak, but the gods
Are strong, and their laws stronger still.
Because of laws, we believe in gods,   800
And we live determining right and wrong.
It's up to you, if the law will be corrupted,
And they go unpunished who murder guests
Or dare to plunder temples of the gods,
Then, there is no justice for men.   805
Believing such crimes a disgrace, avenge me.
Pity me. Stand back
Like a painter and view my sufferings,
A queen once, but now your slave;
Fortunate in children once, now old, and childless, too;   810
City-less, deserted, most miserable of mortals.

No, no, where are you turning your step?
You'll do nothing, it seems. O my misery!

Why do we mortals labor for other knowledge
And search everything as we should,   815

Hecuba | 209

But Persuasion, the queen of the arts,
We don't struggle at all to learn well.
By paying a Sophist a fee, we could learn
How to get whatever we happen to want.
Why then should anyone hope to succeed?   820

I no longer have children, a ruin myself,
A spear-captive for dirty chores.
I see the smoke of my city leap up.
(Perhaps this part of my argument will prove useless:
Bringing in Aphrodite. Nevertheless, it must be said.)   825
My mantic daughter lies by your side,
Whom the Phrygians call Cassandra.
Where will you show your happy love, my lord?
What thanks for the dearest embraces in bed
Will my child get, or I, too?   830
In the darkness and charm of the night,
Mortals have their greatest pleasure.
Listen: You see this dead man?
Doing right by our family connection,
You do right by him. My argument misses   835
One thing: if my voice were in my arms
Or hands or hair or bottom of my feet
By Daedalus' skills or some god's,
How everything would hold your knees,
Crying out every word there is.   840
My master, O great light of Greece,
Do this! Put forth your avenging hand
For an old woman, although she's nothing—still!
The good man serves justice,
And punishes the bad—always.   845

CHORUS:
A mystery how all things fall out for mortals,

And the laws of necessity draw the line,
Turning the worst enemies into friends,
Making those once gentle into enemies.

AGAMEMNON:
I pity you and your child and your misfortunes,   850
Hecuba, and your suppliant hand.
For the sake of gods and men, I want to bring
This unholy man to justice for you,
If it seems right to do well by you
And not appear to the army to favor Cassandra   855
To plot this death on a Thracian lord.
One thing bothers me:
The army sees this man a friend
And the dead man an enemy. If he's *my* friend,
That's no business of the army.   860
Think of this: You have me
Sympathetic, eager to help you,
But reluctant to challenge the Achaeans.

HECUBA:
Good god!
There is no mortal who is free.
Either one is a slave for money or for fate.   865
Or a city mob or written laws
Keep him from using his resolution.
Since you fear—and care—so much for the mob,
I shall set *you* free—from fear.
Join me if I plot a crime   870
In killing this man, but don't *do* it.
If there's any outburst from the Achaeans
Or aid for the Thracian suffering what he will,
Stop it, without seeming to do it for *me*.
Have no fear. I shall set the rest right.   875

Hecuba

AGAMEMNON:
How then? What will you do? Taking a sword
In your old hand kill a barbarian man?
By poison? With what help?
Whose hand is with you? Where are your friends?

HECUBA:
This roof conceals a mob of women.   880

AGAMEMNON:
You mean these captives, hunted down by Greeks?

HECUBA:
With them I shall avenge myself on my murderer.

AGAMEMNON:
How shall women have power over men?

HECUBA:
Numbers are terrifying, unconquerable with a plot.

AGAMEMNON:
Terrifying, but I have doubts about the women.   885

HECUBA:
Why? Did women not kill Aegyptus' sons,
Not depopulate Lemnos of men completely?
Let it be so here. Enough talk.

(Pointing to a SERVANT.)

Send that woman safely through the army
For me. Go say to my Thracian host,   890

"Hecuba, once queen of Troy, summons you—
Your business no less than hers—and your sons.
Your children must hear her words."
Agamemnon, hold back the funeral rites
For the newly killed Polyxena, so brother   895
And sister will be one fire, a double care
For a mother, and covered with earth.

AGAMEMNON:
So it shall be. If the army could sail,
I could not give you this favor.
But now no god sends favoring winds.   900
We must calmly wait a chance to sail.
May it turn out well. All agree:
For each one and his city: That evil
Shall suffer some evil, and the good prosper.

(AGAMEMNON and attendants with bier exit.)

CHORUS:
O fatherland of Ilium,   905
No longer will you be called unsacked,
Such a cloud of Greeks covers you,
Wastes you, spear by spear,
Your crown of towers   910
Cut down, most pitifully stained,
Defiled by ash.
O ruined town I shall no longer haunt you.

I was destroyed at midnight,
When after my dinner, sleep spread sweetly   915
On my eyes, and song, dance were done,
Sacrifices, too,

My husband sleeping.
His spear was hung upon its peg.   920
He could not see
The many sailors stepping on Troy's shore.

I was arranging in the net
My curls to bind my hair,
Gazing into the boundless gleam of a golden mirror,   925
Upon the sheets about to fall in bed.
A cry rose to the citadel.
This call went through Troy city:
"Children of the Greeks, when,   930
When will you wreck Troy's acropolis
—And go to your home!"

I left my loving bed, half-nude
Just like a Spartan girl.
Praying before blest Artemis. Wretched me got
        nothing.   935
I saw my husband killed, and I was taken
Out on the bitter sea. I turned
And looked upon the city
As the ship sped homeward,   940
Cutting me off from the Trojan land
—I fainted in sorrow.

A curse on Helen, sister of the Dioscuri, and the
        Idaean shepherd,
Monstrous Paris,   945
Since he tore me from my native land.
Their marriage, that was not a marriage, forced me
From my home, some revenge from hell.
May the sea not take her back,   950
May she never find her fatherland!

(POLYMESTOR enters with his TWO SONS.)

POLYMESTOR:
O Priam, most beloved of men, and you
Beloved Hecuba, I weep seeing you
And your city and your daughter just killed.   955
What misery!
Nothing can be trusted: Not good reputation.
Not doing right, for that ends badly.
The gods mix things back and forth,
Adding in an uproar so we might honor them
In ignorance. But why lament things   960
That get us nowhere in the face of evil?

But if you blame my absence, hold off.
I was away in the interior mountains of Thrace
When you came here. As I arrived,
Your servant met me hurrying   965
Here already from my home.
She spoke your words, and I came to hear.

HECUBA:
I am ashamed to look on you directly,
Polymestor. I am in such trouble.
Before one who saw me prosperous, I'm ashamed   970
To be seen fallen in this misfortune I'm in now,
And I can't look at you with steady eyes.
Don't consider it ill will,
Polymestor. Besides, custom blames
Women who look directly at men.   975

POLYMESTOR:
No wonder. But what do you want of me?
Why have you called me from the house?

HECUBA:
I want to say something personal
To you and to your sons. Order
Your attendants to stand away from the tent.   980

POLYMESTOR:
You may go! This place is safe unattended.
You are a friend, and the Achaean army
Is my friend. But you must tell me
What a fortunate man can do to help
An unfortunate friend. I am at your service.   985

HECUBA:
First tell me of my son, Polydorus, whom you
        have
At home from my hand and his father's:
If he lives. I shall ask other things after.

POLYMESTOR:
Most certainly he does. *He* is fortunate.

HECUBA:
Dearest friend, your words are worthy of you.   990

POLYMESTOR:
What else do you wish to know?

HECUBA:
If he remembers anything about his mother?

POLYMESTOR:
Secretly, he wants to come here to you.

HECUBA:
Is the gold he came with from Troy safe?

POLYMESTOR:
Safe. Under guard in my house. 995

HECUBA:
Save it now. Don't desire what is your neighbors.'

POLYMESTOR:
Never. Let me enjoy my own, lady.

HECUBA:
Do you know what I shall say to your children?

POLYMESTOR:
I don't. You will reveal it in your speech.

HECUBA:
My dear friend, how I love you now! There are . . . 1000

POLYMESTOR:
What do I and my sons need to know?

HECUBA:
. . . Ancient caves of Priam's gold.

POLYMESTOR:
You wish me to tell your son this?

HECUBA:
Indeed, if you are a religious man.

POLYMESTOR:
Why must my children be here? 1005

HECUBA:
It's better, if you die, that they know.

POLYMESTOR:
Well said. Wiser, too.

HECUBA:
Do you know the House of Trojan Athena?

POLYMESTOR:
The gold is there? What's the landmark?

HECUBA:
A black rock rising above the ground.   1010

POLYMESTOR:
You want to tell me anything else?

HECUBA:
I want you to save the gold I brought.

POLYMESTOR:
Where? Hidden in your robe?

HECUBA:
It is stored in the tent among the war spoils.

POLYMESTOR:
Where? These are Achaean fortifications for the
        ships.   1015

HECUBA:
The tents of the Trojan women are separate.

POLYMESTOR:
Is it safe inside? Empty of men?

HECUBA:
No Achaeans. Just us alone.
But come in the tent. The Argives yearn
To loosen the sail ropes homeward from Troy.   1020
After you do all you must, you can go back
With your children to where you house my son.

(HECUBA, POLYMESTOR, and his TWO SONS exit.)

CHORUS:
You haven't yet paid the penalty—but you will, justly.
Like someone falling into a harborless sea,   1025
You shall fall far short of your heart's desire,
Wrecking your life. Where a violation
To human and divine justice meet,   1030
The outcome is deadly, deadly.
Greed's path will cheat you and has sent you
Condemned by death to hell, you wretch,
Leaving life by an unsoldierly hand.

(Within.)

POLYMESTOR:
Horrible! I'm blinded, my poor eyes gone!   1035

CHORUS:
Did you hear the Thracian's lament, my friends?

POLYMESTOR:
And worse horror: my children, your terrible slaughter!

CHORUS:
O friends, more crimes are worked in the house.

POLYMESTOR:
But you won't run off and escape.
Bashing, I shall break the inside of the tent.   1040
See—my strong hand pounds like a weapon

CHORUS:
Shall we go after him? It's time to help
As allies Hecuba and the Trojan women.

(HECUBA enters.)

HECUBA:
Strike, spare nothing, bash down the house,
You won't bring light to your eyes,   1045
Nor will you see your children I have murdered.

CHORUS:
Have you really brought down the Thracian,
Overpowered the host, done what you say?

HECUBA:
You will see him now in front of the tent,
A blind man going blindly on crazy feet,   1050
See the bodies of the two children I killed
With the help of the best Trojan women. He paid
My price. He comes, you see, from the tent.
But I'm going out of the way, keeping back
From the great, unconquerable, raging-mad Thracian!   1055

(POLYMESTOR enters on all fours.)

POLYMESTOR:
What torture! Where go? Where stand? Where put in?
Shall I take the way of a four-foot beast

Of the mountains, on my hands tracking some quarry,
This way, turning that way,   1060
Longing to take the man-murdering Trojan women
Who ruined me?
An outrage, an outrage, these Trojan women,
Most hideous,
In what corner do they shiver in fear?   1065

God of the Sun, if you would heal, heal
The bleeding lids of my eyes
And free my blind sight.
Ah! Ah!

Quiet! I hear that silent step of women.
Where shall I strike   1070
And eat their meat and bones,
A banquet for wild beasts,
Winning payback,
For my brutal mutilation?

Poor me. Where shall I drift, leaving my wasted
          children   1075
To be torn apart by these bacchantes from hell,
Slaughter for dogs, a wild dinner of blood,
Mountain exposure?

Where stand? Where go? Where turn,
Gathering my linen robe, like a ship   1080
With its cables furls its sail,
Guardian of my children, rushing to their bed of
          death?

CHORUS:
Wretched man, terrible misfortune is yours   1085

For your horrible and abysmal crimes.
A god has dealt heavily with you.

POLYMESTOR:
O, help, men of Thrace
Famous for horses, the lance-bearing people,   1090
Ares' own.
Help, Achaeans! Help, Sons of Atreus!
I cry, cry, cry out!
O come, come for the gods' sake.
Does anyone hear, no one help? What are you doing?
Women have destroyed me,   1095
Captive women!
I have suffered horribly, horribly—
What disgrace!
Where shall I turn? Where shall I go?
Where flying high over heaven's roof   1100
Orion or Sirius throws out
The burning light of his eyes, or miserable   1105
Shall I be driven into the strait of black hell?

CHORUS:
It is excusable, when one suffers or endures so much
Horror, to free oneself from a wretched life.

(AGAMEMNON enters.)

AGAMEMNON:
Hearing a cry, I came. It was not calm Echo,
Child of the mountain rock, ringing   1110
Through the army. If we didn't know
The Trojan towers had fallen to the Greek spear,
This uproar would have terrified us completely.

POLYMESTOR:
O my beloved Agamemnon, I know you, hearing
Your voice. You see my suffering?   1115

AGAMEMNON:
Ugh!
Polymestor, poor man, who ruined you?
Who blinded your eyes, gouged the sockets,
And killed these children? Whoever it was
Had great hate for you and your sons.

POLYMESTOR:
Hecuba with the captive women   1120
Destroyed me, no, more than destroyed.

AGAMEMNON:
What? You did this, as he says?
You, Hecuba, dared this bold act?

POLYMESTOR:
What do you mean? Is she nearby?
Speak, tell me where she is, so I can   1125
Grab her, tear her apart, rip her flesh.

AGAMEMNON:
You, what is wrong?

POLYMESTOR:
                    By the gods, I beg you,
Let me set my raging hand upon her.

AGAMEMNON:
Wait. Put aside the barbarian from your heart.

Speak, so hearing you and her in turn,   1130
I may judge justly your tragedy.

POLYMESTOR:
I will. There was a Polydorus, youngest son
Of Priam and Hecuba, whom his father, Priam,
Gave me to raise in my house,
Surely suspecting Troy's fall.   1135
I killed him. Why did I kill him?
Listen, how it was wise foresight.
I was afraid the child would remain your enemy.
Regather the Trojans and reunite the city.
The Achaeans, knowing a son of Priam alive,   1140
Would raise an army again against Troy,
Then ravage and plunder my Thracian plains.
Troy's neighbors would fare badly,
Right where we suffer now, my lord.

Hecuba, knowing the deadly fate of her son,   1145
Led me on with a story that she would tell me
Of chests of Priam's gold in Troy.
She brought me alone into the tent with my
        children,
So no one would know what she did.
I sat in the middle of a couch, knees bent.   1150
Many Trojan women sat on both sides
Of me, as if I were a friend,
And examined my robe in the light
And praised the Edonian weaving. Others,
Seeing my two Thracian spears, stripped   1155
Me naked, both of arms and clothes.
All the mothers, marveling at the children,

Rocked them in their arms away
From their father, passing them on.

After what seemed a calm greeting—suddenly   1160
Some took swords somewhere out of their robes
And stabbed my children. Others, taking
Enemy revenge, held down my hands
And legs. Wanting to help my children,
If I raised my face, they held   1165
Down my hair. If I moved my hands,
Wretched me could do nothing in the mob of women.

At last, an outrage beyond outrage,
They committed an atrocity: taking their brooches,
They stabbed, gutted my poor eyes.   1170
Then they fled throughout the tent,
And I attacked them, like a beast
Who harassed murdering dogs,
Searching every hole, like a hunter,
Hurtling, thrashing.

                    I did you this favor   1175
And suffered because I killed your enemy,
Agamemnon. To be brief:
If anyone spoke badly of women before,
Or speaks now or will speak,
I shall sum up their speech: 1180
Neither earth nor ocean nourishes such a race.
So everyone knows who has met one.

CHORUS:
Don't be rash! Don't censure like this

The whole female race by your experience.
[We are many. Some are hated.   1185
Some born to the order of evil.]

HECUBA:
Agamemnon, men's tongues should
Not be stronger than their acts.
But he who does well should speak well.
Or if he does wrong, his words ought to be hollow,   1190
And he unable to gloss over injustice.
Some wise men are perfect at this,
But they can't last to the end
And they wreck themselves. No one ever escaped.
My introduction was for you. Now   1195
I turn to him and answer his words.

You who say you freed the Achaeans from more pain
And killed my son for Agamemnon's sake!
But, O most cowardly of men,
The barbarians never were friends of Greeks,   1200
Nor could be. What favor were you eager
To do? To contract some marriage?
Are you a kinsman, or would get some advantage?
The Greeks would ravage your land, sailing back?
You think to persuade someone of this?   1205
The gold, if you want to speak truth,
Killed my son and your greed.
If not, why, when Troy prospered,
And the towers stood about the citadel,
And Priam lived and Hector's spear flourished,   1210
Why not then, if you really wished to do
This favor, raising the child in your own house,
Kill him, or bring him living to the Argives?
But when our light had failed, and with smoke

The city signaled its fall to the enemy,   1215
You killed a guest who came to your hearth.

Hear now how you are revealed a coward.
If you really are a friend of the Achaeans,
You should have given the gold, which you claim
Was not yours, but his, and brought it   1220
To those who needed it so far from home.
Even now you don't let it out of your hands,
Hoarding it still in your house.
If you raised my son as you should
And saved him, you would have a great reputation.   1225
Good friends show themselves best in times
Of trouble, while luck always has friends.
If you needed money and my son was well-off,
My son's treasury would have been yours.
Now you don't have him for a friend,   1230
The gold is useless, your children gone,
And you like this!

                    I tell you, Agamemnon,
If you help him, you show yourself a coward.
He was neither pious nor trustworthy, where he
            should
Have been, not holy nor just, treating well a guest.   1235
We'll say you favor the wicked, being so yourself.
But I rebuke my master no more.

CHORUS:
Yes! Yes! For mortal men, good deeds
Create speeches of good words.

AGAMEMNON:
It is hard for me to judge another's wrongdoing,   1240

But I must. For he bears the shame
Who takes this matter up and casts it off.
So you may know: I don't think you did me,
Or even the Achaeans, a favor killing a guest,
But to possess the gold in your house.   1245
You say what you need to, being in trouble.
Perhaps to you killing a stranger is trivial.
But this is horrible to us Greeks.
How can I judge you not guilty?
I can't. Since you dare to do what   1250
Is horrible, endure what is ugly.

POLYMESTOR:
What! It seems I'm less than a slave woman
And held to account by the contemptible.

HECUBA:
Is it not just, since you did wrong?

POLYMESTOR:
My children and my eyes—for the gods' sake!   1255

HECUBA:
You suffer? And me? I don't suffer for a child?

POLYMESTOR:
You rejoice proudly over me, you bitch?

HECUBA:
Should I not rejoice in my vengeance?

POLYMESTOR:
Soon you won't, when sea water . . .

HECUBA:
. . . Carries me to the coast of Greece?   1260

POLYMESTOR:
. . . Covers you, fallen from the masthead.

HECUBA:
Who will force me to jump?

POLYMESTOR:
You yourself will climb the mast.

HECUBA:
With wings on my back or what?

POLYMESTOR:
You'll become a dog with flaming eyes.   1265

HECUBA:
How do you know my changed form?

POLYMESTOR:
The Thracians' prophet, Dionysos, said so.

HECUBA:
He told you nothing of *your* sad fate?

POLYMESTOR:
No, or you would never have snared me with your
        treachery.

HECUBA:
Shall I die or live here?   1270

Hecuba | 229

POLYMESTOR:
Die. The name on your tomb shall be . . .

HECUBA:
Will you say a verse on my new shape?

POLYMESTOR:
. . . The Sign of the Bitch, a sailor's landmark.

HECUBA:
No matter, since you paid me back.

POLYMESTOR:
And your daughter, Cassandra, must die.   1275

HECUBA:
I spit that prophecy back on you.

POLYMESTOR (pointing to AGAMEMNON):
His wife will kill her, a bitter housekeeper.

HECUBA:
May Tyndareus' daughter not go so mad!

POLYMESTOR:
This man himself she shall take down, raising her ax.

AGAMEMNON:
You, are *you* mad, and love trouble?   1280

POLYMESTOR:
Kill me! A painful bath in Argos awaits you.

AGAMEMNON:
My men, won't you drag him away?

POLYMESTOR:
Does it hurt you to hear it?

AGAMEMNON:
                              Will you stop his mouth?

POLYMESTOR:
Stop it. It is said.

AGAMEMNON:
              Right now
Won't you cast him away on some desert island,   1285
Since he is so bold-mouthed?

Hecuba, poor woman, go bury
Your two corpses. Trojan women,
You must go to your masters' tents.
Already I see the winds leading home.   1290
May we have good sailing and see happily
Our homes, setting aside this trouble.

CHORUS:
Go to harbors and tents, my dear friends.
Endure your slave-work.
It is iron necessity.   1295

              (All exit.)

Notes

3. *Polydorus.* Son of Hecuba and Priam, killed in the Chersonese by King

Polymestor. The Greeks dreaded the unburied corpse; until it was buried, the soul (ghost) could not enter the Land of the Dead. (Cf. *Iliad*, 1.4–5, and Sophocles, *Antigone*.)

4. *Phrygian*. Trojan.

7–8. *Thrace. Chersonesean plateau*. The Hellespont in northern Greece. The Modern Dardanelles at the entrance to the Black Sea in Turkey. The Chersonese, the "dry island" (peninsula), forms the western shore of the Hellespont strait, where, in World War I, the Battle of the Dardanelles (1915) was fought. A strategic area and Greek meeting ground for a clash of civilized and barbarian values.

24. *child of Achilles*. Neoptolemos killed Priam at the altar where Priam had gone for sanctuary. The altar had been built by Apollo and Poseidon so the atrocity was double. The play is based on atrocities.

25–27. A sacred bond protected guest and host, presided over by Zeus *Xenios* ("Protector of Hospitality"). Polymestor's crime of killing his guest Polydorus out of greed, and casting the body into the sea, rather than burying it, would be triply heinous in Greek eyes. *Philoxenía* is the sacred law of hospitality. Cf. line 715. *Polymestor* ironically means "man of many counsels or plots." Cf. Odysseus as "man of many counsels" in the *Odyssey* 2.173, etc.

36. *Peleus' son*. Achilles. In the *Sack of Troy*, the Greeks sacrifice Polyxena on the tomb of Achilles. The introduction of the ghost of Polydorus at the beginning of the play helps us accept the ghost of Achilles here and his request for the sacrifice of Polyxena, which is essential for the unity of the plot.

53. Agamemnon is the leader of the Greek army.

59–97. Hecuba's first solo song (monody). Greek anapests. Usually, Greek poets use dialogue in iambic trimeters (six iambics) at this point in the play, but Euripides, "the Irrationalist" (Dodds), often makes extensive use of songs, indicative of his highly emotional plays. The music is lost.

68–75. The ancients believed that dreams were prophetic.

87–88. *Helenus. Cassandra*. Hecuba's son and daughter, both prophets. Cassandra has become the mistress of Agamemnon.

98–152. Parodos (entrance of the chorus). Choral ode.

103. *Achaean*. Greek.

113. *Danaans*. Greeks.

123. *Sons of Theseus*. Acamas and Demophon, sons of the legendary king of Athens, Theseus.

133. *Son of Laertes*. Odysseus.

137. Persephone was a goddess of the underworld.

145. To balance the heroic code, suppliancy functioned as a way for the weaker to have protection against the stronger. The suppliant was supported by Zeus *Heketesios* ("Of the Suppliants") (Adkins, *Merit*, 65, 80.). Cf. line 345.

154–176. Hecuba's second solo song.

176–196. Lyric duet. Note how the alternating passages, especially the single-line alternations (stichomythia), raise the tension of the scene, here and later in the play.

188. *Argives.* Greeks.

197–215. Polyxena's song.

216–443. First Episode.

239–241. In the *Odyssey* (4.240–264), Helen, demonstrating her innocence during the Trojan War, claims, probably falsely, that Odysseus visited her and she abetted his escape. Hecuba's involvement is not mentioned and may be an invention of Euripides.

254–257. During the fifth century, the controversial Sophists ("wise men") taught rhetoric, the art of persuasive speech. Euripides, though associated with them, has Hecuba criticize their methods here, as does Plato (e.g., in the *Gorgias* and *Protagoras*). Later (814–820), Hecuba will praise rhetoric. Indeed, her successes and failures will depend heavily upon the art of persuasive speech in the rest of the play. The same can be said of Odysseus, who sways the assembly, and Polymestor ("of many counsels") in the final scene. Many connections exist between tragedy and oratory. (Cf. lines 1189–1194.)

269. *Tyndareus' daughter.* Helen.

292. In democratic Athens, but not in Homeric times, laws were equal for all (principle of *isonomía*).

325. Mount Ida is a range of mountains near Troy.

338. *Nightingale.* See the introduction.

361. *Hector.* Trojan hero and brother of Polyxena.

388. *Thetis' Son.* Achilles.

441. *the Dioscuri.* Castor and Polydeuces, brothers of Helen, later deified and protectors of sailors.

444–483. First Stasimon (Choral Ode). 444–454: Strophe A. 455–465: Antistrophe A. 466–474: Strophe B. 475–483: Antistrophe B. The chorus often changes the perspective from that of the characters. Unlike Hecuba and Polyxena, who lament their conditions of death and slavery, the chorus speculates on where they are going and what Greek festivals they might participate in, though they conclude by reiterating Polyxena's metaphor of marrying Hades, Death himself. Euripides' choruses often invoke a far place by longing to escape present pain (cf. *Bacchae*, 402–416). Here the transmigration is more complex, invoking the beautiful ceremonies of Greece but participating as a slave.

450. *Doric*. Peloponnesian, in the south of Greece.

451. *Phythian*. Phythia, the land of Achilles, was in northern Greece.

455–465. Delos is a Greek island and was the center for the worship of Apollo and his twin sister, Artemis. Leto, mother of the twins, was said to have held on to a certain palm tree at their birth. That tree became an object of worship. Euripides joins it with the laurel, sacred to Apollo. In 426 BC, Athens controlled Delos and reestablished the festival that occurred every four years, a year that may help date the play.

466–474. At the Panathenaia, a celebration of Athena, after whom Athens was named, a robe was carried to her wooden statue in the Erectheum on the acropolis in Athens. The garment represented Zeus' victory over the Titans. Here it includes Athena's chariot and horses. The procession appears on the Parthenon Frieze.

484–628. Second Episode. The description of Polyxena's death (518–582) to appease the ghost of Achilles and hence bring the Greek army prosperous winds to journey back to Greece recalls Iphigeneia's, her sister's, sacrifice at Aulis by her father, Agamemnon, to stir the winds that brought the Greek army first to Greece. Cf. Euripides' *Iphigenia at Aulis*. Female heroism is common in Euripides. So is questioning the gods.

485. *Ilium*. Troy.

509. *The two sons of Atreus*. Agamemnon and Menelaus, husband of Helen.

555–556. Editors agree that the needless repetition indicates that these lines are spurious.

629–656. Second Stasimon. 629–637: Strophe. 638–646: Antistrophe. 647–656: Epode. Shifting perspective again to add variety to the tale, the chorus recalls the ironically simple causes of the great tragedy of the Trojan War and the horrors of its aftermath, even sympathizing with Greek victims.

631. *Alexandros*. Paris.

641. The river Simois flowed by Troy.

651. *Eurotas*. The main river in Sparta.

657–904. Third Episode.

684–725. A kommós, a lament between the chorus and Hecuba, with the chorus keeping to the iambic trimeters of the dialogue, while Hecuba by contrast sings lyrically in Greek dochmiacs (⌣ — — ⌣ —) to indicate her erratic emotions.

685. *bacchic.* Dionysian, belonging to Dionysos. Here, wild with grief. Hence the dochmiacs.

715. Philoxenía. Cf. note to 25–27.

808. An old tradition claims that Euripides was a painter once. (Barlow, *The Imagery of Euripides*, 15).

816–820. On the use and theory of rhetoric in this play, cf. note to 254–257.

886–887. The fifty daughters of Danaus stabbed to death all but one of the fifty sons of Aegyptus, his brother, who, after being rejected as suitors, pursued them from Egypt to Greece. Cf. Aeschylus, *The Suppliants*. The women of Lemnos killed all but one of the men, who had turned to concubines (the Lemnian Horror). Cf. Euripides' *Hypsipyle* (fragments). A foreshadowing of events to happen in the play, the bonding of the women is key here.

905–951. Third Stasimon. 905–913: Strophe A. 914–922: Antistrophe A. 923–932: Strophe B. 933–942: Antistrophe B. 944–951: Epode. The chorus now takes a more personal view and domesticates the tragedy.

952–1055. Fourth Episode.

1056–1108. A *kommós*, lyric lament between actor and chorus. Polymestor's song in the ecstasy of dochmiacs (⌣ — — ⌣ —). Chorus responds in calmer iambic trimeters. Cf. note to 684–725.

1076. *bacchantes.* Followers of Dionysos.

1091. *Ares.* The god of war.

1100–1103. *Orion.* A giant hunter, blinded by Oenopion and Dionysos, for trying to assault Oenopion's daughter, Merope, he went to Lemnos, where he was cured by the beams of the rising sun. Hence Polymestor's earlier appeal to the sun to cure his blindness (1066–1068). His great dog is *Sirius*, the Dog-Star, the brightest star in the sky, which is in the constellation Canis Major ("greater dog"), southeast of Orion's constellation. Sirius brings on the scorching "dog days" of late summer (cf. *Iliad*, 22.29). Images of dogs and hunting permeate the play, as in Polymestor's prophecy for Hecuba (1265–1273).

1109–1295. Exodos. The "trial" of Hecuba. Note the oratory of the law courts. We also find here the *agon* (debate) and *rhesis* (the set, reasoned, speech). One of the questions that arises here is what is a legitimate claim and legitimate bond between human beings. Note the discussion between Odysseus and Hecuba earlier in the play (234–302) and the themes of suppliancy and the guest/host obligations.

1127. Dropped lines like this are called *antilabé* in Greek. They promote intensity.

1154. *Edonian*. The Edoni were a Thracian tribe. Thrace was famous for its weaving.

1185–1186. Spurious lines.

1200. *barbarians*. Ancient Greeks saw themselves as superior to other races, like the Medes and Persians, who were considered "barbarians," "speaking gibberish" ("bar"-"bar"-ians). Being Trojan, Hecuba herself would be considered a barbarian.

1259–1279. Polymestor prophesies the violent death of Hecuba and Agamemnon. Hecuba will go mad in the shape of a dog and drown at sea, while Agamemnon, along with his concubine, Hecuba's mantic daughter, Cassandra, will be murdered by his wife, Clytemnestra, the sister of Helen of Troy. The course of destruction begun by Paris' abduction of Helen continued into the action of this play and beyond.

1273. *The Sign of the Bitch*. Cynossema, a headland near Thrace. Euripides might have made up this story of Hecuba's death and associated her with this landmark. Mossman thinks not (*Wild Justice*, 35–36).

1278. *Tydareus' daughter*. Clytemnestra, wife of Agamemnon and sister of Helen.

1281. *Argos*. In the southern Peloponnesus, here the land of Agamemnon.

1290. The favorable winds may echo the favorable winds after the sacrifice of Iphigenia at Aulis.

Appendix: Elements of Greek Tragedy

Greek tragedy forges powerful emotion and complexity of thought. Its actions can be the most violent imaginable. Actions that many cultures avoided mentioning publicly the Greeks put on the stage: matricide, patricide, infanticide, incest, madness, suicide, and mutilation. To balance the atrocities and avoid disgust, Greek drama employed formal elements that gave aesthetic distance and acceptability to its plots. Sometimes the plays even ended happily. Such controlled shock had an exportability, a clarity, and a relevance that fascinated many later civilizations.

Like later Western theater, its conventions derived from religion. At first, Greek drama was a celebration and rite of the god Dionysos. Etymologically, "tragedy" means the "goat song" sung at the sacrifice of a goat and perhaps was the dithyramb (hymn to Dionysos) or the satyr play (a burlesque) honoring that god. The use of masks and the acting may have originated in attempts to become Dionysos. This worship of the Greek god evolved into more secular theater, but the antiphon (verse and chorus) between priest and congregation continued in the form of the actors and chorus. As in the Christian commemoration of the Crucifixion, violence was offstage; messengers related to the audience the tragic action. Plays marked certain festivals during the Greek year, such as the three-day spring City

Dionysia, and were not confined to Athens. Each dramatist had a day to present four plays, three tragedies in a trilogy, connected or not connected, and a lighter drama (satyr play). They were competitive, and prizes were awarded.

In the beginning (the sixth and early fifth century BC), song and dance dominated. Much effort and expense, at a cost to rich citizens, was needed for the training of the chorus. The perhaps legendary Thespis is said to have invented the play form: one actor responding to the choral odes. Aeschylus added a second actor and Sophocles a third. The first actor is called the protagonist, the second the deuteragonist, and the third the tritagonist, after the *agon*, contest or struggle, in the plays (cf. English "agony"). The "three-actor rule" may have resulted from the difficulty of following too many actors in masks. But masks allowed actors to take on multiple roles. Later tragic plots became more central than choral odes. Men acted all the parts.

Plays were performed in the day, outdoors, not in the cave-like darkness of modern theaters. Tragedy was public drama: Five thousand spectators with a strong sense of community watched in the open air. The actors stood, perhaps on a slightly raised platform, before a one-story wooden building (*skené*, our word "scene," literally, "tent") with a door, sometimes representing a palace. Inside was the *eccyclema*, a wheeled platform (5′ x 7′) and prop. Entrances were on both sides and through a door in the center.

The chorus (twelve, or later fifteen, members) danced and sang to the double pipe (aulus) on the orchéstra, the (circular, rectangular, or trapezoidal?) dancing space in between the action and the audience, who watched from raised seating in the *theatron*, "the seeing place." It should be kept in mind that the audience always sees the chorus in front of the action. Most of the music and all the choreography have been lost. The chorus was a unique institution. The meter changes from dialogue to various sung lyric forms, though the chorus leader speaks his part. The choral odes have two or three stanzas: strophe (turn), antistrophe (counterturn), and sometimes epode (after-song). Strophe and antistrophe correspond metrically. Choral songs signal a shift in perspective. The chorus was often the concerned voice of society reacting to the action. They are usually conservative, holding to old-school views (and older poetic forms) in the age of fifth-century intellectual disruption. They voice traditional folk wisdom and echo old Olympian religious views that create tension by jarring against the complexities of the hero's action—like Polonius. They can generalize a situation into traditional mythology as well as accent the emotion for the audience. They can take sides and give advice, but they are not the guide to final interpretation. The choragos, leader of the chorus, can act as an actor in an episode.

In addition to masks, which allowed actors to assume more than one role, the actors wore raised footwear and elaborate costumes. They often sang "monodies" or duets. There may be a *kommós*, a lament shared by actor and chorus. Later attempts in Renaissance Italy to recapture Greek tragedy invented opera, which is similar to Greek tragedy in its formality and its alternation of rhythmic recitation and song. The dialogue was in double iambic trimeters ($\smile — \smile — \smile — \smile — \smile —$), a line of six feet. A long syllable may be substituted for a short syllable in the first, fifth, ninth, and last position. Greek meter measured the length of the syllable, not stress as in English. A long syllable had twice the duration of a short syllable, as in music two quarter notes equal a half note. The state paid the actors. The winner wore the ivy of Dionysos.

The form of Greek drama, including comedy, usually took the following pattern with few variations, alternating action and choral song (cf. the later five-act play):

Prologue (spoken by one or more characters)
Parodos (choral ode sung by the chorus entering the theater
   through the "side passages," *parodoi*)
First Episode (dialogue and action between the actors)
First Stasimon (choral ode)
Second Episode
Second Stasimon
Third Episode
Third Stasimon
Exodos (final scene after the last stasimon)

Throughout the plays, the conscious and elevated use of rhetoric, the high style, is evident. But the sections of the play gave variety to the expression of language and changed the point of view. Sometimes, to vary the drama, the action among the characters alternated with lyric passages. The chorus often related the action to more general patterns of myth or turned the action into image and metaphor. Messenger speeches often provided a more distanced view of the action. Dialogue could be emotionally intensified by shifting from long speeches to single sword thrusts of alternating lines (*stichomythia*) or to dropped lines (*antilabé*—i.e., split between characters). At times, the language shifted to a debate (*agon*), an essay (*rhesis*), or a story (messenger speech). Each shift could shorten or extend the aesthetic distance between character and action. A messenger, for example, may be an outside observer telling a short story whose vivid aural power stirs the audience's imagination, while an agonist might lament his or her life. A god could be brought down on a crane over the stage.

Most tragedies use older mythological tales for their plots, often the Trojan War or the royal House of Thebes. Like the language, the action and the characters are thus elevated above the quotidian. The plots may scrutinize the old Homeric code in the light of the new city-state (polis), shifting between that heroic world and contemporary urban life. They concern themselves with problems within the family, between family and state, and problems in marriage. They also focus on women, fate, free will, morality, foreigners, and identity. The heroes or heroines often seek revenge or knowledge, and they sometimes journey to self-knowledge. Usually, they end in defeat and death, but not without demonstrating great courage and resolution in a conflict with fate. Often the plays interrogate and complicate more than easily resolve conflicts. The protagonist courageously suffers in a mysterious web of nature, society, and the divine. In *The Poetics*, Aristotle pointed out that tragedies gain power from an anagnorisis (recognition or discovery) and a peripety (reversal of fortune) (1449a). He also thought that tragedy stimulates fear and pity in the audience (1452a) and ends with a final cartharsis (emotional cleansing; release from tension) for the audience (1449b). Overall, we can add that tragedy transforms another human being's pain into order, pleasure, and, in the largest sense of the term, beauty.

Suggestions for Further Reading

For classical references in general, see *The Oxford Classical Dictionary*, 4th ed., ed. Spawforth, Hornblower, and Eidinow, 2012.

*Adkins, A. W. H. "Basic Greek Values in Euripides' *Hecuba* and *Hercules Furens*." *Classical Quarterly* 16 (1966): 193–219.

———. *Merit and Responsibility: A Study in Greek Values*. 1960. Reprint, Chicago: University of Chicago Press, 1975.

Arnott, W. G. "Euripides' Newfangled *Helen*." *Antichthon* 24 (1990): 1–18.

*Arrowsmith, William. "Euripides' Theatre of Ideas." 1964. Reprinted in *Euripides: A Collection of Critical Essays*, ed. Erich Segal, 13–33. Englewood Cliffs, NJ: Prentice-Hall, 1968.

Barlow, Shirley A. *The Imagery of Euripides*. 3rd ed. London: Bristol Classical Press, 2008.

Bieber, Margarete. *The History of the Greek and Roman Theater*. 2nd ed. Princeton, NJ: Princeton University Press, 1961.

Blondell, Ruby. *Helen of Troy: Beauty, Myth, Devastation*. Oxford: Oxford University Press, 2013.

Burnett, Anne Pippin. *Catastrophe Survived: Euripides' Plays of Mixed Reversal*. Oxford: Oxford University Press, 1971.

———. "*Trojan Women* and the Ganymede Ode." *Yale Classical Studies* 25 (1977): 291–316.

*Conacher, D. J. *Myth, Theme and Structure in Euripidean Drama*. Toronto: Toronto University Press, 1967.

* Entries marked by an asterisk are basic reading.

Craik, Elizabeth. "Sexual Imagery in *Troades*." In *Euripides, Women, and Sexuality*, ed. Anton Powell, 1–15. London: Routledge, 1990.

Croally, N. T. *Euripidean Polemic: The "Trojan Women" and the Function of Tragedy*. Cambridge: Cambridge University Press, 1994.

Diggle, James. *Euripidea*. Oxford: Oxford University Press, 1994.

———. *Studies on the Text of Euripides*. Oxford: Oxford University Press, 1981.

*Dodds, E. R. "Euripides the Irrationalist." 1929. Reprinted in *The Ancient Concept of Progress*, 78–91. Oxford: Oxford University Press, 1973.

Gellie, G. H. "*Hecuba* and Tragedy." *Antichthon* 14 (1980): 30–44.

*Gilmartin, Kristine. "Talthybius in the *Trojan Women*." *American Journal of Philology* 91 (1970): 291–316.

*Goff, Barbara. *Euripides: Trojan Women*. London: Duckworth, 2009.

Gregory, Justina. *Euripides and the Instruction of the Athenians*. Ann Arbor: University of Michigan Press, 1991.

*Grube, G. M. A. *The Drama of Euripides*. London: Methuen, 1941.

Halleran, Michael. *Stagecraft in Euripides*. Totowa, NJ: Barnes & Noble, 1985.

Havelock, Erik A. "Watching the *Trojan Women*." In *Euripides: A Collection of Critical Essays*, ed. Erich Segal, 115–127. Englewood Cliffs, NJ: Prentice-Hall, 1968.

*Hughes, Bettany. *Helen of Troy: Goddess, Princess, Whore*. New York: Knopf, 2005.

*Jaeger, Werner. "Euripides and His Age." In *Paideia*, I, trans. Gilbert Highet, 332–357. Oxford: Blackwell, 1939.

Kennelly, Brendan. *Euripides' "Trojan Women."* Newcastle upon Tyne: Bloodaxe, 1993.

Kip, A. Maria van Taalman. "Euripides and Melos." *Mnemosyne* 40 (1987): 414–419.

Kitto, H. D. F. *Greek Tragedy*. 3rd ed. London: Methuen, 1961.

Kovacs, David. *Euripidea*. Leiden: Brill, 1994. Biographical sources with translations.

———. *Euripidea Altera*. Leiden: Brill, 1996. Discussions of Greek texts.

———. *Euripidea Tertia*. Leiden: Brill, 2003. Discussions of Greek texts.

———. *The Heroic Muse: Studies in the "Hippolytus" and "Hecuba" of Euripides*. Baltimore: Johns Hopkins University Press, 1987.

Lardinois, André, and Linda McClure, eds. *Making Silence Speak: Women's Voices in Greek Literature and Society*. Princeton, NJ: Princeton University Press, 2001.

Lefkowitz, Mary R. *Women in Greek Myth*. Baltimore: Johns Hopkins University Press, 2007.

Lesky, Albin. *Greek Tragedy*. Translated by M. Dillon. New Haven, CT: Yale University Press, 1983.

Lloyd, Michael. *The Agon in Euripides*. Oxford: Clarendon Press, 1992.

———. "The Helen Scene in Euripides' *Troades*." *Classical Quarterly* 34 (1984): 303–313.

Lloyd-Jones, Hugh. *The Justice of Zeus*. 2nd ed. Berkeley: University of California, 1983.

Maguire, Laurie E. *Helen of Troy from Homer to Hollywood*. Oxford: Wiley-Blackwell, 2009.

Mastronade, Donald. *The Art of Euripides: Dramatic Technique and Social Context*. Cambridge: Cambridge University Press, 2010.

McHardy, Fiona. *Revenge in Athenian Culture*. London: Duckworth, 2008.

*Meridor, Ra'anana. "Hecuba's Revenge." *American Journal of Philology* 96 (1978): 28–35.

*Michelini, Ann Norris. *Euripides and the Tragic Tradition*. Madison: University of Wisconsin Press, 1987. Contains a history of Euripidean scholarship (pp. 131–180 on *Hecuba*).

Mossman, Janet, ed. *Oxford Readings in Classical Studies: Euripides*. Oxford: Oxford University Press, 2003.

*———. *Wild Justice: A Study in Euripides' "Hecuba."* Oxford: Clarendon Press, 1995.

Munteanu, Dana LaCourse. "The Tragic Muse and the Anti-Epic Glory of Women in Euripides' *Troades*." *Classical Journal* 106 (2011): 129–147.

Murray, Gilbert. "Euripides' Tragedies of 415 B.C.: The Deceitfulness of Life." *Greek Studies* (1946): 127–148.

*———. *Euripides and His Age*. 2nd ed. Oxford: Oxford University Press, 1965.

*Nussbaum, Martha C. *The Fragility of Goodness: Luck and Ethics in Greek Tragedy and Philosophy*. Rev. ed. Cambridge: Cambridge University Press, 2001. (pp. 397–421 on *Hecuba*.)

Osofisan, Femi. *Women of Owu*. Ibadan: University Press, 2006. African adaptation of *Trojan Women*.

Perdicoyanni, Hélène. *Commentaire sur les Troyennes d'Euripide*. Athens: Editions Historiques Stefanos Basilopoulos, 1992.

Phillips, David D. *Avengers of Blood: Homicide in Athenian Law and Custom from Draco to Demosthenes*. Stuttgart: Steiner, 2008.

*Poole, Adrian. "Total Disaster: Euripides' *Trojan Women*." *Arion* 3 (1976): 257–287.

Rabinowitz, Nancy Sorkin. *Anxiety Veiled: Euripides and the Traffic in Women*. Ithaca, NY: Cornell University Press, 1993.

Roisman, Hanna, ed. *The Encyclopedia of Greek Tragedy*. 3 vols. Chichester: Wiley-Blackwell, 2014.

Sartre, Jean-Paul. *Les Troyennes*. Paris: Gallimard, 1965. French adaptation. English version: Duncan, Ronald. *The Trojan Women*. New York: Knopf, 1967.

———. "Why the *Trojan Women*?" 1965. Reprinted in *Euripides: A Collection of Critical Essays*, ed. Erich Segal, trans. Jeffrey Mehlman, 128–131. Englewood Cliffs, NJ: Prentice-Hall, 1968.

Scodel, Ruth. *The Trojan Trilogy of Euripides*. Göttingen: Vandenhoeck & Ruprecht, 1980.

Segal, Charles. *Euripides and the Poetics of Sorrow: Art, Gender, and Commemoration in "Alcestis," "Hippolytus," and "Hecuba."* Durham, NC: Duke University Press, 1993.

Segal, Erich. "Euripides: Poet of Paradox." *Oxford Readings in Greek Tragedy*, ed. Erich Segal, 244–253. Oxford: Oxford University Press, 1983.

Seneca. *"Troades": Text, Translation and Commentary*. Edited by Elaine Fantham. Princeton, NJ: Princeton University Press, 1982.

*Sidwell, Keith. "Melos and the *Trojan Women*." In *Trojan Women: A Collection of Essays*, ed. David Stuttard and Tamsin Shasha, 30–44. York: Actors of Dionysos, 2001.

Skutsch, O. "Helen, Her Name and Nature." *Journal of Hellenic Studies* 107 (1987): 188–193.

*Stanford, W. B. *Greek Tragedy and the Emotions*. London: Routledge, 1983.

Stevens, P. T. *Colloquial Expressions in Euripides*. Weisbaden: Steiner, 1976.

Stuttard, David. *An Introduction to "Trojan Women": Including an Adaptation of the Play*. Brighton: Company Dionysos, 2005.

Vellacott, Philip. *Ironic Drama*. Cambridge: Cambridge University Press, 1975.

Walton, J. Michael. *Euripides Our Contemporary*. Berkeley: University of California Press, 2010.

*Webster, T. B. L. *The Tragedies of Euripides*. London: Methuen, 1967.

West, M. L. *Immortal Helen*. London: Bedford College, 1975.

Index

Index | 249

WISCONSIN STUDIES IN CLASSICS

Patricia A. Rosenmeyer, Laura McClure,
Mark Stansbury-O'Donnell, and Matthew Roller

Series Editors

The Classical Epic Tradition
John Kevin Newman

Ancient Anatolia: Aspects of Change and Cultural Development
Edited by Jeanny Vorys Canby, Edith Porada, Brunilde Sismondo Ridgway,
    and Tamara Stech

Euripides and the Tragic Tradition
Ann Norris Michelini

*Wit and the Writing of History: The Rhetoric of Historiography
    in Imperial Rome*
Paul Plass

*The Archaeology of the Olympics: The Olympics and Other Festivals
    in Antiquity*
Edited by Wendy J. Raschke

Tradition and Innovation in Late Antiquity
Edited by F. M. Clover and R. S. Humphreys

The Hellenistic Aesthetic
Barbara Hughes Fowler

Hellenistic Sculpture I: The Styles of ca. 331–200 B.C.
Brunilde Sismondo Ridgway

Hellenistic Poetry: An Anthology
Selected and translated by Barbara Hughes Fowler

Theocritus' Pastoral Analogies: The Formation of a Genre
Kathryn J. Gutzwiller

Rome and India: The Ancient Sea Trade
Edited by Vimala Begley and Richard Daniel De Puma

Kallimachos: The Alexandrian Library and the Origins of Bibliography
Rudolf Blum
Translated by Hans H. Wellisch

The Matter of the Page: Essays in Search of Ancient and Medieval Authors
Shane Butler

Greek Prostitutes in the Ancient Mediterranean, 800 BCE–200 CE
Edited by Allison Glazebrook and Madeleine M. Henry

Sophocles' "Philoctetes" and the Great Soul Robbery
Norman Austin

Oedipus Rex
Sophocles
A verse translation by David Mulroy, with introduction and notes

The Slave in Greece and Rome
John Andreau and Raymond Descat
Translated by Marion Leopold

Perfidy and Passion: Reintroducing the "Iliad"
Mark Buchan

*The Gift of Correspondence in Classical Rome: Friendship in Cicero's
    "Ad Familiares" and Seneca's "Moral Epistles"*
Amanda Wilcox

Antigone
Sophocles
A verse translation by David Mulroy, with introduction and notes

Aeschylus's "Suppliant Women": The Tragedy of Immigration
Geoffrey W. Bakewell

Couched in Death: "Klinai" and Identity in Anatolia and Beyond
Elizabeth P. Baughan

Silence in Catullus
Benjamin Eldon Stevens

Odes
Horace
Translated with commentary by David R. Slavitt

Shaping Ceremony: Monumental Steps and Greek Architecture
Mary B. Hollinshead

Selected Epigrams
Martial
Translated with notes by Susan McLean

The Offense of Love: "Ars Amatoria," "Remedia Amoris," and "Tristia" 2
Ovid
A verse translation by Julia Dyson Hejduk, with introduction and notes

Oedipus at Colonus
Sophocles
A verse translation by David Mulroy, with introduction and notes

Women in Roman Republican Drama
Edited by Dorota Dutsch, Sharon L. James, and David Konstan

Dream, Fantasy, and Visual Art in Roman Elegy
Emma Scioli

Agamemnon
Aeschylus
A verse translation by David Mulroy, with introduction and notes

*Trojan Women, Helen, Hecuba: Three Plays about Women
and the Trojan War*
Euripides
Verse translations by Francis Blessington, with introductions and notes

Echoing Hylas: A Study in Hellenistic and Roman Metapoetics
Mark Heerink